SPECIAL MINISTER
of
HOLY COMMUNION
Certificate of Commissioning

This is to Certify

That _____

was commissioned a

SPECIAL MINISTER
of
HOLY COMMUNION

according to the Rite of the Roman Catholic Church

on the _____ day of _____

in the year _____ at _____ .

Let us pray to God our Father that

_____

chosen to administer the Body of Christ,
may be filled with His blessing.

_____
Dated

_____
Pastor

A Handbook for Eucharistic Ministers

An Important Office
of
Immense Love

Joseph M. Champlin

PAULIST PRESS
New York/Ramsey

ACKNOWLEDGEMENTS

Scripture texts are taken from *New American Bible*, copyright © 1970, by the Confraternity of Christian Doctrine, Washington, D.C. and are used by permission of the copyright owner. All rights reserved.

Excerpts from the English translation of *The Roman Missal* © 1973, International Committee on English in the Liturgy, Inc. (ICEL); excerpts from the English translation of *Rite of Anointing and Pastoral Care of the Sick* © 1973, ICEL; excerpts from the English translation of *Holy Communion and Worship of the Eucharist Outside Mass* © 1974, ICEL; the English translation of the *Rite of Commissioning Special Ministers of Holy Communion* © 1978, ICEL. All rights reserved.

NIHIL OBSTAT
Rev. J. Robert Yeazel
Chancellor
Censor Librorum

IMPRIMATUR
+ Francis J. Harrison
Bishop of Syracuse

September 1, 1979

The Nihil Obstat and Imprimatur are official declarations that a book or pamphlet is free of doctrinal or moral error. No implication is contained therein that those who have granted the Nihil Obstat and Imprimatur agree with the contents, opinions or statements expressed.

Cover and interior art: Ann Dalton
Graphics: Tim McKeen

Library of Congress
Catalog Card Number: 80-80085

ISBN: 0-8091-2287-1

Published by Paulist Press
Editorial Office: 1865 Broadway, New York, N.Y. 10023
Business Office: 545 Island Road, Ramsey, N.J. 07446

Printed and bound in the
United States of America

Contents

Introduction

This book has been designed for both newly appointed eucharistic ministers and those who have fulfilled that function for a considerable period of time.

For recently designated religious or lay individuals, it offers the historical background of this development within the Church, a process for selecting ministers, and several practical "how-to" chapters which deal with the distribution of the consecrated bread, handling the cup, bringing our Lord to the sick and leading a Communion service when no priest or deacon is available.

For the veteran special minister, that material may be somewhat familiar and unnecessary, although as a review even those sections could be helpful. However, three other chapters deal with the inner qualities of the eucharistic distributor and these, I hope, should possess somewhat more permanent value.

One contains testimonies from several experienced ministers on the impact that their appointment and the exercise of this responsibility has exerted upon them. A second describes in some detail the characteristics of a good eucharistic minister—prayerful, faith-filled, and joyful. The last includes suggestions about regular prayer periods in preparation for the discharge of this task. We envision this book thus as something of a manual for repeated use by a minister of Holy Communion.

For the pastor, other priests and parish leadership people, Chapter 6, "A Parish Formation Program," may prove particularly useful. It sketches rather fully an actual evening of preparation for new appointees sponsored in one large suburban church and then adds several further general suggestions for such programs. They should also find valuable the recommendations for the selection of ministers found in Chapter 3.

The idea for this book came from Mr. Donald F. Brophy, the managing editor at Paulist Press, who urged me to undertake the task. Unfortunately, my heavy pastoral responsibilities kept the project in the category of those good, desirable tasks we want to tackle, but for which we never seem to find the time.

Paulist Father George R. Fitzgerald, also an editor at the company, picked up the idea two years later, and his encouragement plus the availability of some added moments in my schedule gave me the push I needed.

I am grateful to both of them for their ideas, confidence and technical assistance. Moreover, I wish to thank: two long-standing friends for their support, Fathers J. Murray Elwood and John Roark; Father Dennis Hayes for his aid with Chapter 6; the eucharistic ministers at my former parish of Holy Family in Fulton, New York for their inspiring example as well as their reflections which made up Chapter 4; Mrs. Pat Gale who typed the manuscript with swiftness and accuracy.

A young layman well educated in theology and

working as a top executive within one diocesan church structure commented the other day on just how much his own faith in the Eucharist had been deepened through serving as a minister of Communion. His reaction, I know, parallels the experience of many throughout this country and beyond. May the pages which follow facilitate that growth process and help those called to such an "important office"[1] to realize ever more clearly that the gift they touch so often is the wonderful gift of the Eucharist, the greatest gift of all, a testament of Christ's "immense love."[2]

Roots in the Past

The custom of lay persons distributing the Holy Eucharist to others may have become a relatively well-established practice in your parish or worshiping community. On the other hand, your appointment and that of others to this sacred ministry could be a pioneering step in the area, a giant leap for both priests and parishioners.

Within the past decade throughout the United States religious and lay persons in ever increasing numbers have been designated by local bishops to serve in this capacity. Because religious sisters and brothers as well as the laity have been so chosen, we prefer to term them special rather than lay ministers of Communion.

Reaction to the new procedure has not been universally positive. While no innovation receives unanimous acceptance, the introduction of others besides the priest as eucharistic distributors seems to have engendered more than the usual amount of opposition. A relatively recent national survey indicated that only about forty-five percent of American Roman Catholics endorsed the practice of special ministers for Communion. On the contrary nearly seventy-five percent expressed approval of earlier controversial moves like vernacular liturgies, altars facing the people, guitar music and the sign of peace.

The most commonly articulated criticism runs something like this:

"I was always taught that only the sacred, anointed hands of a priest are allowed to touch the host. In fact, we were admonished never to reach for the particle, even if the celebrant dropped one during the rush of distribution. I don't like this new approach, especially when the person is an ordinary lay person, not even a sister or a nun."

In the memory of modern-day Catholics, having special ministers of Communion is a new procedure, but ten years represent only a moment in the long history of our ancient Church. Most cannot recall anyone but ordained priests and deacons distributing the host in our life spans prior to a decade ago.

Nevertheless, according to actual history, the simple practice is another new, yet old procedure which has been restored to meet the liturgical needs of our day.

HISTORICAL DEVELOPMENT

Jesuit Father Joseph Jungmann's massive volume, *The Mass of the Roman Rite,* has long been judged our most comprehensive and accurate history of the liturgy. In that text he describes the various procedures for receiving Communion which have been customary over the twenty centuries of Catholic tradition.[1]

Up until the fourth century it was a rule, not merely an ideal that the faithful communicate at every Mass. Believers understood clearly that the action of all receiving the Lord's body and blood formed an integral and natural part of every eucharistic celebration. Nevertheless, priests normally celebrated only on Sundays.

As a consequence, the faithful both communicated at that Sabbath Eucharist and also took a sufficient supply of sacred particles home with them for the week ahead. There these early believers carefully preserved the consecrated bread, consumed a portion of it day after day before eating their regular food, and gave a particle to others.

This practice of lay persons—or, more specifically here, those not priests or deacons—keeping the sacred particles within the home thus made it likewise possible for the sick, prisoners and isolated monks to communicate frequently, even daily despite the fact that weekday Mass was then a rarity.

It is also very evident from historical research that lay persons ordinarily received the Lord directly into their hands for the first nine centuries. Writings, pictures, and documentation speak of or illustrate this practice.

ST. CYRIL, BISHOP OF JERUSALEM

For example, the most widely quoted proof of this assertion is an instruction which St. Cyril, the bishop of Jerusalem, issued on the Sunday after Easter in 348. Speaking to a group of adults received into the Church but a few days earlier, he outlined the proper method for receiving our Lord in Communion.

> When you approach (Communion) do not come with your hands outstretched or with your fingers open, but make your left hand a throne for the right one, which is to receive the King. With your hand hollowed receive the body of Christ and answer Amen. After having, with every

7

precaution, sanctified your eyes by contact with the holy body, consume it, making sure that not a particle is wasted, for that would be like losing one of your own limbs. Tell me, if you were given some gold dust, would you not hold it very carefully for fear of letting any of it fall and losing it? How much more careful, then, you should be not to let fall even a crumb of something more precious than gold or jewels! After receiving the body of Christ, approach the chalice of his Blood. Do not stretch out your hands, but bow in an attitude of adoration and reverence, and say Amen (*Mystagogic Catechesis* V, 21, 1–22, 4).[2]

A little bit later St. Theodore of Mopsuestia (d. 428) offered this commentary: "Everyone stretches out his right hand to receive the Eucharist, which is given, and puts his left hand under it."

A century or so after that, St. John of Damascus (d. 570) observed: "Making the figure of the cross with our hands, we receive the body of Christ crucified."

Finally, even as late as the ninth century, a sacramentary or altar book contained a Communion scene showing the Eucharist placed in the hand of the communicant.

The practice, thus, of lay persons touching, holding and distributing the consecrated bread has deep roots in our Catholic past. In fact, we can maintain with good backing that such activities were more common than not throughout the first eight or nine centuries of the Church.

CHANGE: MIDDLE AGES

For very complex reasons the pattern then changed, and handling or distributing the Eucharist became a practice more and more reserved for the clergy alone.

Was this shift mainly a result of abuses, of sacrilegious or irreverent use of the consecrated particles by lay communicants or distributors?

Some contemporary critics who have opposed the restoration of Communion in the hand or the re-establishment of lay ministers for the Eucharist argue in this fashion. However, the historical data does not seem to support that objection. There were clearly occasional abuses and even an official decision or two addressed to those situations. But other testimonies in the Middle Ages reveal various irreverent incidents even when Communion was placed directly on the tongue.

The more substantive causes behind the change which restricted distributors to clerics alone appear to be different developing attitudes about the Eucharist itself and our liturgical worship.

In those medieval days many Christians began to emphasize the divine aspects of the Eucharist and to stress the real, holy, tremendous, awesome presence of Christ our God in the sacrament. The host was, in a way, to be adored more than to be eaten. Our unworthiness in the face of this sublime gift led to less frequent reception of Communion, a greater distance between altar and pew, and more cautions surrounding the celebration of Mass.

Concurrently in those centuries the laity were gradually eliminated from the liturgy, even from the "sacred places," like the altar, which became reserved territories for clerics and in some cases for priests alone.

In fact during the eighth and ninth centuries lay persons were almost totally excluded from public worship. The priest alone stood at the altar and at an ever increasing distance from the congregation; the laity no longer brought offerings to the altar within the Mass, but were required to do so beforehand; singing was done by a special schola or small choir only; the general intercessions disappeared; the faithful now could not see what was happening on the altar because the celebrant blocked their view; the canon or eucharistic prayer was said quietly; everything took place in silence or in a language less understood by the people.

For any Catholic fifteen years or older, all of that sounds quite familiar and reminds us of the Church we grew up in and which held sway as late as the 1950's and 1960's.

This brief historical overview, although simplified and thus necessarily incomplete, nevertheless provides us with a background of understanding behind many popular traditions or principles in pre-Vatican II Catholicism:

"The wedding Mass is one of the rare occasions you as a lay person are allowed in the sanctuary." "Never chew the host." "One should always be silent in God's house." "Make sure you go to confession before going to Communion."

These notions grew out of a frame of reference which developed at the end of the first millennium and differed in many ways from the approaches followed in the first centuries of Catholicism. Those medieval concepts obviously were handed down very carefully to us by our forefathers of the faith. They had value, respected one aspect of the mystery which is the Eucharist, and should not be casually disregarded.

In the next chapter we will trace some of the movements or steps—official and unofficial, from both below and above—which have reversed, as it were, the process. These grass roots efforts and Roman documents gave theological bases and practical impetus for restoring the laity's part in liturgy. Special ministers of Communion, including lay men and women, are a natural outgrowth of that trend as well as a pragmatic solution to a pastoral problem.

Lord, I Am Not Worthy

At the end of the last century, several European monasteries began to look at their liturgies and ask questions. Common sense, loving concern and historical research indicated that the then current style of worship left something to be desired. The monks at Solesmes, Beuron, Maria Laach and Louvain, among others, consequently attempted to discover and recover some of the better liturgical practices of the past.[1]

The reforms they encouraged naturally had a monastic orientation, but at Klosterneuberg in Austria, Father Pius Parsch sought to apply the fruit of this new thinking and ancient research to parish life. His pastoral efforts were to be the inspiration for many similar labors in Europe and the United States, including those of Monsignor Martin B. Hellriegel at Holy Cross Church, St. Louis.

TWENTIETH CENTURY BEGINNINGS

Such grass roots suggestions soon received papal approval and support. St. Pius X in 1903 issued a decree on sacred music which called for reforms in that sphere, and also urged involvement of lay persons in the sacred liturgy.

In a classic, pivotal, oft-quoted statement, the Holy Father declared the "most important and indispensable source" of "the true Christian spirit" is the faithful's "active participation in the most sacred mysteries and in the public and solemn prayer of the Church."[2]

That ushered in, officially, a totally new trend: restoring the faithful, the laity, to their rightful place in worship and calling upon all present to be active participants.

The first half of our century witnessed a constant interplay between a push from below for further reforms in the liturgy and a prod from above which changed various rituals.

Catholics began to receive Communion at an earlier age and were encouraged by papal directives to approach the sacred table frequently, even daily.

Liturgical reformers pleaded for what many termed revolutionary, even heretical innovations: an altar facing the people, vernacular liturgies, lay persons reading the Scriptures, Holy Week services at hours more in conformity with their original times. The proponents often faced opposition or rejection or ridicule.

THE MYSTICAL BODY OF CHRIST

However, in 1943, Pope Pius XII issued an encyclical on "The Mystical Body of Christ" which came to serve as the theological basis for these various liturgical reforms. It spoke of the Church as the mystical body of the Lord and thereby highlighted the dignity of each member.

To that effect, Pius cites words of St. Leo uttered centuries earlier: "Recognize, O Christian, your dignity, and being made a sharer of the divine nature go not back to your former worthlessness along the way of unseemly conduct. Keep in mind of what Head and of what body you are a member." [3]

Membership in this Church not only gives each Christian a unique dignity, it also binds us together with one another. Pope Pius viewed the Mass as giving special evidence "of our union among ourselves and with our divine Head, marvelous as it is and beyond all praise."[4]

That dignity and closeness, that rightful place of lay persons in worship, nevertheless, does not in any way diminish the singular position of the priest or his importance for the liturgy. "In this act of sacrifice, through the hands of the priest, whose word alone has brought the immaculate Lamb to be present on the altar, the faithful themselves with one desire and one prayer offer it to the eternal Father. . . ."[5]

MEDIATOR DEI

Dignity; participation; bond with one another; community; priesthood: these concepts were taken up in detail a few years later, in 1947, by the same pontiff in his encyclical letter *Mediator Dei* on "The Sacred Liturgy."

The following excerpt has particular relevance for any person who has been appointed as a special minister of Communion: "By the waters of baptism, as by common right, Christians are made members of the mystical body of Christ the Priest, and by the 'character' which is imprinted on their souls they are appointed to give worship to God; thus they participate, according to their condition, in the priesthood of Christ."[6]

The many and varied changes introduced by the Church in the post-World War II years and prior to the Second Vatican Council in one way or another simply flow from these fundamental notions.

For example, a mitigation of the eucharistic fast rules removed obstacles which in modern times had kept the laity from Communion. Introduction of the vernacular promoted participation by the congregation in word and song. Reversal of altars brought priest and people closer together as a family, a community, a mystical body in worship.

VATICAN II: LITURGICAL REFORM

On December 4, 1963 these scattered half-century official and unofficial reform movements were tied together by publication of the *Constitution on the Sacred Liturgy.*

The Council Fathers understandably brought out once more those key notions of the lay person's participation and dignity: "Mother Church earnestly desires that all the faithful should be led to that full, conscious and active participation in liturgical celebrations which is demanded by the very nature of the liturgy. Such participation by the Christian people as 'a chosen race, a royal priesthood, a holy nation, a redeemed people' (1 Peter 2:9, see 2:4–5), is their right and duty by reason of their baptism."[7]

They likewise underscored the community nature of liturgy: "It is to be stressed that whenever rites, according to their specific nature, make provision for communal celebration involving the presence and active participation of the faithful, this way of celebrating them is to be preferred, so far as possible, to a celebration that is individual and quasi-private."[8]

Finally, the Vatican Council document once and for all indicated that not only the priest, but others have a true function to perform. A totally clerical liturgy should be an experience of the past: "In liturgical celebrations each person, minister or layman, who has an office to perform should do all of, but only, those parts which pertain to his office by the nature of the rite and the principles of liturgy."[9]

The revised ritual books published after the Council—for Mass, the sacraments, the Church year, the Liturgy of the Hours—faithfully follow the principles of reform enunciated in that *Constitution on the Sacred Liturgy*. The Order of Mass, to illustrate, makes provision for Communion under both kinds.

Nevertheless, there was no explicit mention made in the Constitution or in the Order of Mass of special or lay ministers for distribution of the Eucharist. However, as the number of communicants multiplied because of the reforms noted above, and as the availability of priests, deacons or acolytes diminished because of deaths or resignations, the need for such persons developed.

DOCUMENTS ISSUED BY PAUL VI

On January 29, 1973 Pope Paul VI issued an instruction *Immensae Caritatis* on "Facilitating Sacramental Communion in Particular Circumstances."[10] In that document the Holy Father said: "First of all, provision must be made lest reception of Communion become impossible or difficult because of insufficient ministers."

Paul VI envisioned two situations in which such a lack of adequate personnel could exist: either during or outside Mass. The commentary by our Bishops' Committee on the Liturgy spells this out in detail:

> a. when there is a large number of regular communicants at the parochial liturgy and a shortage of ordinary ministers to assist the president of the assembly in the distribution of the Eucharist. A shortage of eucharistic ministers, in such a case, causes the Communion rite to be out of proportion to the total celebration. The goal is not, however, to shorten or have more efficient Masses, but to give them their proper value and to avoid the rush it takes to distribute Communion to everyone present.

> b. when outside Mass the ordinary minister is impeded from fulfilling his office due to age, bad health, or other pastoral demands;

> c. when there is a shortage of ordinary ministers of the Eucharist (e.g., in some mission countries where the catechist has traditionally led the Sunday prayer service when no priest, deacon, or acolyte was present).[11]

Several months later the Holy See published a section of the Roman Ritual entitled *Holy Communion and Worship of the Eucharist Outside of Mass.* It reflected the development and official approval of special or lay ministers for Holy Communion by providing rituals "if the minister is not a priest or deacon" and for "administration of Communion and Viaticum to the sick by an extraordinary minister."[12]

In some ways, you are not worthy to be or become a special, extraordinary lay or religious minister of Holy Communion. No one is. Nor is any person worthy to serve as a deacon, priest, bishop or pope.

AN OFFICE OF IMMENSE LOVE

In his instruction endorsing ministers like yourself Pope Paul VI described the Eucharist as a testament of Christ's "immense love," a "wonderful gift," "the greatest gift of all," and insisted that "the greatest reverence toward this sacrament be constantly maintained."[13] We thus can never display adequate reverence for Holy Communion nor bring to the altar appropriate holiness.

However, from the perspective outlined in this chapter, as a Catholic lay person or religious who has received the sacraments of initiation—baptism, confirmation and the Eucharist—you do have the fundamental dignity or worthiness to serve in that function. Moreover, the Church in its authoritative decrees has been calling for greater participation in the liturgy, a less clergy-dominated worship, more distribution of roles, and, now, even appointment of the laity as extraordinary eucharistic ministers. Finally, in your own parish or worshiping community, the leadership people have judged that it needs these ministers and recommended you as a suitable candidate. The bishop, to complete this process, has approved, in writing, their choice.

Lord, I am not worthy—true; but, on the other hand, I have been selected by a careful process, accomplished presumably with prayer to the Holy Spirit, and appointed by a successor to the apostles.

Precisely how a minister of Communion is or might be so chosen will be the topic we now examine.

17

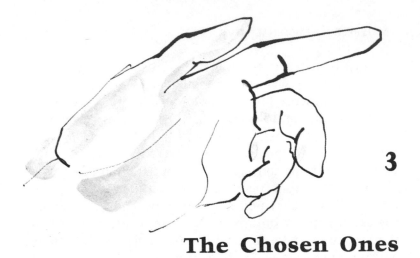

The Chosen Ones

During his preaching ministry, Jesus experienced deep pity within himself when he viewed great crowds of people and the lack of adequate spiritual shepherds for them. He said as a consequence to his followers: "The harvest is good but laborers are scarce. Beg the harvest master to send out laborers to gather his harvest."[1]

But our Lord also did something about the situation. In the very next verse of St. Matthew, we read: "Then he summoned his twelve disciples and gave them authority to expel unclean spirits and to cure sickness and disease of every kind. . . ." Jesus sent these men on mission.[2] Christ thus chose some helpers for his task of proclaiming the good news.

In St. Luke's account, we note that prior to selecting his chosen twelve special assistants, the Savior "went out to the mountain to pray, spending the night in communion with God. At daybreak he called his disciples and selected twelve of them to be his apostles."[3]

Perhaps Jesus did some consultation prior to selection of the twelve, but ultimately he made the choice on his own. In St. Mark's description: "He then went up the mountain and summoned the men he himself had decided on, who came and joined him. He named twelve as his companions whom he would send to preach the good news; they were likewise to have authority to expel demons."[4]

As we know, not all of the twelve chosen ones remained faithful. After our Lord's resurrection and ascension, the Christian community in Jerusalem, about 120 strong and, significantly, under Peter's leadership, decided that another person should take the deceased Judas' office. "It is entirely fitting, therefore, that one of those who was of our company while the Lord Jesus moved among us, from the baptism of John until the day he was taken up from us, should be named as witness with us to his resurrection."

The group followed an interesting selection process to determine who would assume such an important post.

"At that they nominated two, Joseph (called Barsabbas, also known as Justus) and Matthias. Then they prayed: 'O Lord, you read the hearts of men. Make known to us which of these two you choose for this apostolic ministry, replacing Judas, who deserted the cause and went the way he was destined to go!' They then drew lots between the two men. The choice fell to Matthias, who was added to the eleven apostles."[5]

THE EARLY CHURCH GROWS

Later, however, the rapidly growing Church found that the twelve could not handle all of the tasks required for the community's welfare. As the Lord did earlier, the apostles sought assistants who could perform some of their functions.

> In those days, as the number of disciples grew, the ones who spoke Greek complained that their widows were being neglected in the daily distribution of food, as compared with the widows of those who spoke Hebrew. The Twelve assembled the community of the disciples and said, 'It is not right for us to neglect the word of God in order to wait on tables. Look around among your own number, brothers, for seven men acknowledged to be deeply spiritual and prudent, and we shall appoint them to this task. This will permit us to concentrate on prayer and the ministry of the word.' The proposal was unanimously accepted by the community. Following this they selected Stephen, a man filled with faith and the Holy Spirit, Philip, Prochorus, Nicanor, Timon, Parmenas, and Nicholas of Antioch, who had been a convert to Judaism. They presented these men to the apostles, who first prayed over them and then imposed hands on them.[6]

This laying on of hands was the customary Jewish way of designating a person for some task and invoking upon that individual the divine blessing. Moreover, the gesture symbolized a plea asking God to bestow the power necessary to perform this function upon the one chosen.

What Jesus, his apostles and the early Christian community did had a very interesting Jewish precedent centuries earlier with Moses.

After the exodus from Egypt and before entering the promised land, Moses spent considerable time and energy adjudicating conflicts between individuals and small groups among his pilgrim people. Jethro, Moses' father-in-law, with the clearer vision of an outsider, observed the scene, quickly diagnosed how faulty the system of justice had become, and recommended a solution to his daughter's husband.

We find the incident in the Book of Exodus with reference made to it in Deuteronomy.[7] Its parallel to our present-day situation with the appointment of ministers for Communion seems obvious.

The next day Moses sat in judgment for the people, who waited about him from morning until evening. When his father-in-law saw all that he was doing for the people, he inquired, "What sort of thing is this that you are doing for the people? Why do you sit alone while all the people have to stand about you from morning till evening?" Moses answered his father-in-law, "The people come to me to consult God. Whenever they have a disagreement, they come to me to have me settle the matter between them and make known to them God's decisions and regulations."

"You are not acting wisely," his father-in-law replied. "You will surely wear yourself out, and not only yourself but also these people with you. The task is too heavy for you; you cannot do it alone. Now, listen to me, and I will give you some advice, that God may be with you. Act as the people's representative before God, bringing to him whatever they have to say. Enlighten them in regard to the decisions and regulations, showing them how they are to live and what they are to do. But you should also look among all the people for able and God-fearing men, trustworthy men who hate dishonest gain, and set them as officers over groups of thousands, of hundreds, of fifties, and of tens. Let these men render decisions for the people in all ordinary cases. More important cases they should refer to you, but all the lesser cases they can settle themselves. Thus, your burden will be lightened, since they will bear it with you. If you do this, when God gives you orders you will be able to stand the strain, and all these people will go home satisfied."

Moses followed the advice of his father-in-law and did all that he had suggested. He picked out able men from all Israel and put them in charge of the people.

PASTORAL NEEDS TODAY

The circumstances today are similar in many ways.

With fewer priests and many more communicants, the priest at Sunday Masses usually must rush and the people must wait. That wearies the clergy, unduly delays the liturgy and weakens its spiritual effectiveness.

Moreover, the Church urges pastors to see "that an opportunity to receive the Eucharist is given to the sick and aged, even though not gravely sick or in imminent danger of death, frequently and, if possible, daily, especially during the Easter season."[8] With their varied responsibilities and many parishioners, few priests could personally fulfill that ideal. It would be a physical impossibility for them to carry the eucharistic Lord to ten to thirty individuals confined at home more than once a week or even once a month.

Finally, small town parishes, single pastor churches and large communities with many daily Masses frequently find it necessary to cancel a Mass during priests' vacations, retreats, conferences, sickness, and same-day funerals or weddings.

The words of Jethro ring true here. "You will surely wear yourself out, and not only yourself but also these people with you. The task is too heavy for you; you cannot do it alone."

Pope Paul VI in his instruction which approved extraordinary or special ministers of Communion seemed likewise to echo the advice of Moses' father-in-law: "Look among all the people for able and God-fearing people. . . . Thus, your burden will be lightened, since they will bear it with you." With their help Sunday liturgies will flow more reverently and effectively, the sick may receive the Lord more often, and a congregation will have Communion services when the priest cannot be present.

WHAT KIND OF SPECIAL MINISTERS?

Where do we discover those "able and God-fearing persons," "those deeply spiritual and prudent" individuals who will serve as ministers of the sacred bread and cup? How does a parish select them?

The instruction of Paul VI offers some brief guidelines to help us.

This document indicates that the candidates should be sought from the following categories of people and in the order listed: "Reader, student of major seminary, male religious, woman religious, catechist, man or woman."[9]

A concluding sentence in that paragraph adds this qualification to the suggested priority schedule. "This order, however, may be changed according to the prudent judgment of the local ordinary."

In our days during which the Church of the United States has committed itself to involving women more extensively in leadership roles and in the face of such strong desires on the part of many women to exercise those functions, it would seem that the local bishops should adjust that recommended sequence. Their stance might best be to allow the parish community and leaders to determine who are the most suitable candidates without demanding a preference for men or women, religious or lay persons.

SPECIAL ATTENTION TO HANDICAPPED

Following the directions of our American bishops in their November 1978 Pastoral Statement on the Handicapped, special consideration should be given to handicapped persons in the parish. For example, a deaf individual certainly could distribute appropriately both the consecrated bread and the precious blood. Or, to use another illustration, a person in a wheelchair would be able to handle the chalice, even if distributing the hosts might prove awkward. It is not possible to calculate the powerful, positive influence achieved by their mere presence in such leadership and ministry functions before the community. They become teachers and strong symbols simply through being there.

RECOMMENDED QUALITIES

Further on in his instruction, Paul VI lists the qualities which, ideally, should be present in the minister of Communion.

"The person who has been appointed . . . must be duly instructed and should distinguish himself or herself by Christian life, faith, and morals, striving to be worthy of this great office, cultivating devotion to the Holy Eucharist and acting as an example to the other faithful by piety and reverence for this most holy sacrament of the altar. Let no one be chosen whose selection may cause scandal among the faithful."[10]

Selection of the ministers can prove to be an extremely delicate matter for the parish leadership people. Human jealousies and resistance to the very idea of lay persons distributing Communion can make many in the congregation quite critical of the choices.

"Why him?" "I don't understand how he could appoint her." "The pastor, of course, picked his friends and favorites." "Why not me?" Those kind of spoken or unspoken comments will frequently be heard or sensed especially when this program is first introduced at a parish.

The following process has been followed with success on repeated occasions in one parish. It forestalls much of the criticism, engages the community more fully in the selection procedure, preserves the possibility of eliminating a candidate who may be promoted but is unsuitable, and gives the approved ministers a feeling of strong support from the congregation.

SELECTION PROCEDURES

1. Publicize in the parish bulletin that a certain number of persons are needed to function as ministers of Communion. List with this message the qualities given above which Pope Paul VI indicated should be present in the candidate. Invite the members to contact their parish council representative with the name or names of community people they would recommend for the task.

2. Request each parish council delegate to submit to the pastor or pastoral team a certain number of names depending upon the size of the council and the amount of ministers desired. For example, to obtain a dozen ministers from a ten-member council, a request for six names will probably produce sufficient candidates.

3. Tabulate the results, keeping track of who sponsored which individuals. Some persons, probably half of those required, will immediately surface as the choice of several. These are then approved by the pastor or team leaders.

4. Complete the roster by adding the pastor's or the

team's vote to other persons already proposed by council members. In doing this, make sure that each council delegate has as least one of his or her candidates chosen.

To use our illustration: the ten council members will likely suggest between twenty and forty names. About six to eight candidates will be sponsored by two or three people. The pastor or team then adds a vote to four to six other individuals, giving them a total of two or three votes, carefully insuring at that time that each council representative has at least one name in the group of recommended ministers.

If the pastor or team has privileged knowledge about an individual's clear unsuitability, that name can thus be easily dropped without awkwardness.

5. The pastor calls those proposed and seeks their acceptance. If they decline—some always have in my experience—he goes back to the list and, following the procedure in step 4, selects an additional one or ones until the parish has the number needed.

6. Publicize the chosen ones in the parish bulletin and review the general process followed. This indicates that the candidates came forth from the people and the council rather than as the personal selection of the pastor or team.

Once formal appointment has been received from the bishop or his delegate and a training program has been completed, the candidates should be formally commissioned. Rather than commission all at one Sunday Mass, this writer would divide them among all the liturgies at which such ministers are used. In that fashion the seriousness of the selection process, the training program, the episcopal approbation and the task itself will be clearly evident to the congregation as well as to the special ministers.

The Congregation for Divine Worship has prepared formal commissioning rites for a ceremony both during and outside Mass.[11] In addition, it published a simple rite when in necessity a person is designated on the spot for a particular liturgy. These follow.

RITE OF COMMISSIONING
SPECIAL MINISTERS OF HOLY COMMUNION

1. Persons authorized to distribute holy communion in special circumstances should be commissioned by the local Ordinary or his delegate[1] according to the following rite. The rite should take place in the presence of the people during Mass or outside Mass.

A. DURING MASS

2. In the homily the celebrant first explains the reason for this ministry and then presents to the people those chosen to serve as special ministers, using these or similar words:

> Dear friends in Christ,
>   Our brothers and sisters N.* and N. are to be entrusted with administering the eucharist, with taking communion to the sick, and with giving it as viaticum to the dying.

The celebrant pauses, and then addresses the candidates:

1. See instruction *Immensae caritatis I*, nos. 1, 6.
*This reference may be modified according to circumstances.

In this ministry, you must be examples of Christian living in faith and conduct; you must strive to grow in holiness through this sacrament of unity and love. Remember that, though many, we are one body because we share the one bread and one cup.

As ministers of holy communion be, therefore, especially observant of the Lord's command to love your neighbor. For when he gave his body as food to his disciples, he said to them: "This is my commandment, that you should love one another as I have loved you."

3. After the address the candidates stand before the celebrant, who asks them these questions:

Are you resolved to undertake the office of giving the body and blood of the Lord to your brothers and sisters, and so serve to build up the Church?

R. I am.

Are you resolved to administer the holy eucharist with the utmost care and reverence?

R. I am.

4. All stand. The candidates kneel and the celebrant invites the faithful to pray:

Dear friends in Christ,
Let us pray with confidence to the Father; let us ask him to bestow his blessings on our brothers

and sisters, chosen to be ministers of the eucharist:

Pause for silent prayer. The celebrant then continues:

Merciful Father,
creator and guide of your family,
bless + our brothers and sisters N and N.
May they faithfully give the bread of life
to your people.
Strengthened by this sacrament,
may they come at last
to the banquet of heaven.
We ask this through Christ our Lord.

R. Amen.

5. The general intercessions should include an intention for the newly-commissioned ministers.

6. In the procession at the presentation of gifts, the newly-commissioned ministers carry the vessels with the bread and wine, and at communion may receive the eucharist under both kinds.

B. OUTSIDE MASS

7. When the people are assembled an appropriate song is sung. The celebrant greets the people. There normally follows a short liturgy of the Word. The readings and chants are taken, either in whole or in part, from the liturgy of the day or from those given in this rite.

8. The rite continues as above, nos. 2–5.

9. Finally, the celebrant blesses the people and dismisses them in the usual way. The rite concludes with an appropriate song.

RITE OF COMMISSIONING
A SPECIAL MINISTER
TO DISTRIBUTE HOLY COMMUNION
ON A SINGLE OCCASION

10. A person who, in a case of real necessity, is authorized to distribute holy communion on a single occasion[2] should normally be commissioned according to the following rite.

11. During the breaking of the bread and the commingling, the person who is to distribute holy communion comes to the altar and stands before the celebrant. After the Lamb of God the priest blesses him/her with these words:

> Today you are to distribute
> the body and blood of Christ
> to your brothers and sisters.
> May the Lord bless + you, N.

> R. Amen.

12. When the priest has himself received communion in the usual way, he gives communion to the minister of the eucharist. Then he gives him/her the paten or other vessel with the hosts. They then go to give communion to the people.

2. See instruction *Immensae caritatis I*, nos. 2, 6.

4

With Humble
and Contrite Hearts

In the older commissioning rite before the assembled community, the priest reminded the ministers that they "have been chosen for an important office."

Most candidates, in my six years of experience with them at least, hardly need to be reminded of this truth. They often have reservations about accepting the appointment, approach the task with awe, sometimes even with trembling hands, and are profoundly moved by the opportunity.

During the preparation of the bread and wine at Mass, the celebrant whispers "Lord God, we ask you to receive us and be pleased with the sacrifice we offer you with humble and contrite hearts."[1]

The phrase, "humble and contrite hearts," well characterizes the attitude generally expressed by men and women preparing for the task of Communion minister or who have exercised that function for a period of time.

As part of the initial training session it can be very beneficial to provide some moments for the candidates to share with one another how they felt when asked to serve. Later, after the program has been underway in a parish for a year or so and new ministers are being instructed, "veteran" special distributors also could be asked to share their sentiments as they offer the Lord's body and blood to others.

REFLECTIONS OF EUCHARISTIC MINISTERS

I solicited from the special ministers in my former parish brief written reflections upon their own appointment as distributors of Communion and upon their execution of the task itself. Here are edited excerpts from some of these responses with a few words of introduction about each person to place his or her contributions in a more authentic setting.

DEPARTMENT STORE MANAGER

Fran was one of the two original special ministers of Communion at this parish and received the appointment during the early stages of its introduction throughout the United States. A quiet, but active community leader and long-time pillar of the parish, this middle-aged man at that moment served as the manager of a large department store. He always assumed a leadership role in the United Way drive for this city of 15,000 and each Sunday either proclaimed the Scriptures as a lector or took up the collection as an usher. Thus he is a very solid, respected, leadership citizen and parishioner—all of which makes his observations more interesting.

I recall—and probably always will—the Saturday evening our pastor telephoned me requesting that I serve as a lay minister of Communion at Mass the next day. All necessary approval had been obtained from the bishop's office. Due to an illness of the associate pastor, assistance in the distribution of the Eucharist was needed.

As my pastor started to explain the purpose of his telephone call, I became very nervous and even started to perspire. By the time we had completed our conversation, the palms of my hands were moist and beads of perspiration were evident on my forehead. Suddenly to realize that I would be touching the sacred host was overwhelming. As a youngster I served as an altar boy and was taught that only the hands of a priest could touch the body of Christ or any vessels that had contained the Eucharist at one time. To think that I was to be among the privileged few to serve as a lay minister of Communion in the diocese was more than my nervous system could accept.

From the initial day, I became tense, physically weak, and my hands developed a slight tremble as I prepared to touch our Lord's body.

Being one of the first lay ministers, I was subjected to some criticism by my fellow parishioners. On the first occasion, my pastor carefully explained to the congregation the purpose and reason for my serving as a lay minister on that day. I felt he did an outstanding job in his homily explaining that this in no way reflected my being a better or lesser Catholic than any other parishioner. The majority of the parish accepted the change. However, a few members of the parish were critical and voiced their objections to me—even to the point of seeking me out at my place of employment to inform me that they would never receive Communion from me. Fortunately, my pastor had assured the parish that a priest would always be available at every Mass and anyone preferring to receive Communion from a priest would be free to do so. The length of the lines to receive from the priest were always considerably longer than the lay minister's.

When I first started serving, communicants were kneeling at the altar rail, and while this method was more time consuming, I was more comfortable and secure. When the change to standing took place, I was continually aware of the possibility of dropping the host or a particle. As with many changes, once they become familiar, the new methods are more acceptable.

The next change came with the choice of receiving in the hands or on the tongue. Once again, I seemed less nervous when this revision was in effect. Evidently, my emotional system felt that there was safety in numbers—now everyone may touch the host.

I have become much more closer to God. The fact that I, personally, am going to distribute Communion to the other members of our worshiping family makes me feel that I am serving God in a very special, privileged way. While I am not quite so shaky as at the beginning of my service, I still experience a little tenseness and awe, as do many of my fellow lay ministers of Communion.

CORPORATE EXECUTIVE

Jack works for a corporation with many international outlets. He has spent several weeks at a time in Europe and Latin America on business matters, giving him ample occasions to experience the diversities of our universal Church. Nevertheless, he and his wife Kathy, very regular communicants as well as active Catholic school parents and supporters, rather strongly objected to the initial introduction of these special Communion ministers. The note which follows reflects for him and them real inner growth and a true attitudinal conversion.

As you probably know, my first reaction to lay ministers of Communion in the Catholic Church was a negative one.

I guess I still had that feeling the day you called and asked me to become one for our parish.

After thinking about the changes in the Church over the recent years, and following discussions with Kathy regarding these changes, I felt that I also should be able to change to more modern concepts.

I have never regretted that decision. I told you then and still feel that I am not worthy enough to minister Communion to my fellow parishioners, but I cherish the privilege of being able to serve God in this very special way.

I feel that our family has become much closer to God and our Church because of this ministry to Christ.

PHARMACIST

As a pharmacist for thirty to forty years, John has been distributing medicine to thousands. The sixty-year-old needed some of that a decade ago when his health collapsed and he nearly died at the intensive care unit of our local hospital. However, John soon recovered and was back ushering as always at the 8:30 Sunday Mass.

His appointment and this ministry affected him in the same way as it did many others, since these steps ran contrary to years of earlier indoctrination. Offering spiritual medicine to thousands seemed to him more frightening than filling prescriptions at the drug counter.

Years ago, like my father, I received my formal Catholic education at the hands of the Christian Brothers of De LaSalle. These good and dedicated men instilled in me, as they had when my father attended their school, respect for the sanctity of the Catholic Church and, particularly, reverence for the Blessed Sacrament. We were impressed with the fact that only an ordained priest was allowed to touch the Eucharist. As a result of Vatican II many of the precepts that we had been taught as boys seemed in complete disagreement with these new changes in the Church.

When I was asked to serve as a minister of Communion, I judged that I was not deserving to assume this lay function as a result of my early religious education. I felt that there were more deserving people of the parish who should be accorded such a great honor and trust. Perhaps there were parishioners, members of the parish for many years, who might resent a relative newcomer performing this important Church function. I also felt that I should not be a minister of Communion because of the deep emotional effect that it would have on me. Although I was assured that the Lord had been good to me and had spared my life when I was seriously ill, nevertheless the emotional effect on me when I first acted as a minister was tremendous. I felt most honored to act as a minister, but again most humble in doing this wonderful task for the Lord.

Four years have elapsed since I first acted as a lay minister, and this has been a most rewarding and beautiful part of my life. Not only have I been allowed to distribute the Eucharist to my fellow parishioners, but also to my own family, my wife and my daughter.

POWER COMPANY LINEMAN

Bill and his wife—a couple in their thirties—have undergone a spiritual transformation over the past eight years. Alienated from the Church, they found the way home, became involved little by little in parish committees, made a Marriage Encounter, became more involved, and now serve the community in a variety of ways. As a lineman for the power company, the husky husband climbs tall poles and strings electrical wires during the week; on weekends he offers the Lord to parishioners, as now also does his wife Nancy.

The transformation on several levels surfaces in his reflections.

About twenty five years ago as an altar boy I had a very different view of Jesus Christ in the Holy Eucharist. He was a white wafer, large or small; the large one was inscribed with IHS, and, on occasions such as Benediction, enshrined in a golden monstrance for all to adore as the priest elevated it in a cloud of incense; the small ones were distributed to the faithful at Communion.

This was the sacrament that could only be touched by the priest; you couldn't even reach in to dislodge it from the roof of your mouth where it invariably became stuck. Don't chew it; don't touch it; it is sacred; we have gold plates to catch it if it falls and the consecrated hands of the priest to administer it or to retrieve it. God was kept in a gold tabernacle and the wafers were made only by nuns. I always felt quite unworthy to receive the Lord in Communion, and the laws governing the sacrament made it all the more removed from me.

Over the past several years great changes in the sacrament have made Jesus a closer friend. A more relaxed and personal relationship has been formed between us. Jesus used earthen dishes when he consecrated the bread and wine of the Last Supper into his body and blood, not golden cups and platters. He was dealing with common men and he too was a common man. Now he is again reachable and has been brought back to humanness by a Church that feels for its people. With the advent of the bread baked by the people, Communion in the hand and a relaxation of the fasting rules, I believe that Jesus Christ has been put back into our lives on a more personal level than ever before.

To be asked to be a minister of Communion caused me a great deal of consternation. Most of me felt like the altar boy of twenty-five years ago, unworthy to touch the body of Christ, unable to feel a personal relationship to the Holy Eucharist because it was still a very sacred object. At the same time there was an excitement about being put into the position to become more than I had ever been before, to be one of only a few who were thought worthy enough to be a minister of Communion. I was really put into a tough position. All that I had ever been taught about the sacrament from the time I was eight and a novice altar server on one side telling me no and the new more personal, more loving Church that I know today saying that it was acceptable. I felt that I could at least give it a try.

I am very happy now that I decided to try. I feel closer to Jesus Christ and the sacrament of Communion than I ever have before. I feel that I have experienced a change in my attitude toward others and a perceptible change in my own life style. Being on the altar on Sunday and distributing Communion to my family and friends makes me want to be more, to be someone that people can trust and look up to and to do what is right, not just what is convenient or easy. I want to be closer to Jesus through my ministry and closer to others because of it.

FEELINGS OF UNWORTHINESS

One's less than saintly past or youthful follies can be an obstacle for some to accepting their appointment. Walt talks about that and how he worked through those feelings or thoughts of unworthiness, encouraged particularly by the example of St. Augustine.

My first reaction when approached about becoming a lay minister of Communion was very negative. Sure, I have been involved in parish activities through the years, but (that awful *but*) I was no angel in my younger days. Thoughts of my past life with those foolish, shameful and arrogant episodes rose before me. How can I take our blessed Lord into my hands and distribute him to people, many of whom are so much more worthy than I? Yes, I've heard the same question many times, "Well, who is really worthy?"

The lay ministry was first being established in our parish and Father Champlin seemed so convincing. It took a lot of soul-searching on my part. To think: this is God, the almighty Lord of the universe; everything that existed everywhere was created by him. What a thought! And I? I'm nothing, except one of his creations. No!

Well, just a minute. How about some of his saints? How about St. Paul and St. Augustine, especially St. Augustine? He became a great saint after a hectic, sinful life of some twenty years.

During the Second World War while I was in Italy, a copy of *The Confessions of St. Augustine* fell into my hands. I can't remember how, but I was intrigued with his search into the depths of human decadence for the truth which for so many years eluded him. His life, as they say today, was something else.

At any rate, this, perhaps more than anything else, eased me into accepting the honor of being asked.

Father Champlin conducted a little ceremony on that first Saturday at the 5:15 evening Mass. I think there were six of us inducted as lay ministers before the people, a procedure which helped me, and I presume the others, immensely.

During the Mass and as we approached Communion time, I prayed to the Holy Spirit to give me what I needed to carry out my mission. I trembled a bit as I broke the bread into small morsels with the priests and the other lay ministers. The thought of what I was actually doing dawned on me, "This is God the almighty, Lord of the universe"—again that same thought came to me.

Before I knew it, we were in front of the long lines of people and the distribution began. All was proceeding well until, in trying to pick up one of the hosts, a wafer was edged off, falling to the floor. Oh, I thought, why did this happen to me on the very first occasion? Quickly I bent over, picking it up and resuming as calmly as possible. I felt very, very humble and embarrassed until it was all over.

While kneeling, asking forgiveness, I realized that it was accidental, and I've seen it happen to priests, so the remorseful feeling left me.

Later, telling the priest about it, he reassured me that these things do happen sometimes and it certainly wasn't intentional.

Two or three years have passed since then and it hasn't happened to me again.

WIFE, MOTHER, NURSE

Wife, mother of four, registered nurse staffing the local hospital's intensive care unit, Pat found the Church's previous history of not allowing women leadership roles in the sanctuary a source of confusion and doubt as she pondered her own selection.

In response to your request for my feelings and reactions as one of the ministers of Communion, I found it not to be as easy as I thought.

Being a realistic person I try to relate particular happenings in my life to a previous occasion which helps me tie "things" together. Being asked to be a minister of Communion this past July, I cannot relate to *any* prior experience. In turning to Scripture, the story of the woman at the well expressed similar feelings for me (John 4:4–42). The woman inquired, "How can you ask me, a Samaritan and a woman." I too felt: How can I be asked, a lay person and a woman. Being reassured by Jesus' words to her, "If only you recognized God's gift, and who it is that is asking you," I tried to hide personal doubts of unworthiness and accepted. I prayed that my children wouldn't tear the church apart while I was on the altar, and I also asked for patience for their father who felt conspicuous and ill at ease without me in the pew with the family.

Like the woman at the well, partaking in the celebration of Mass as a minister of Communion has intensified the fire of my love for Jesus, allows a quiet time in spiritual reflection just before Mass, and overflows in many little and big ways throughout daily family life.

ARTIST

Another woman, Cathy, an extremely gifted art teacher, found that functioning as a minister of Communion helped her spiritually in several ways, including the elimination of some personal bad living habits.

My first response to becoming a lay minister was rather blasé. I was more concerned with the externals: the how, what, when and what if. I felt privileged though in a prideful sort of way. I didn't realize that people in the parish knew me, let alone know me well enough to nominate me as lay minister. I remember being disturbed with myself for not having all the appropriate feelings of awe that I saw everyone else had.

My first experience also left me with no warm feeling. In fact, with everyone coming at me so fast and trying to remember all the externals, I grew somewhat frightened and was very tempted to back off.

During the past months I have, however, experienced a change not only in feeling but in entire attitude. I don't really know if I can verbally describe the depth of what I feel without it sounding like an exaggeration. Increasingly I have become more respectful and filled with awe, not only in performing this simple act of service, but toward other people. I think I have learned to become more aware of the specialness of each person and perhaps to recognize the Christ in them, whereas I know this is true: that each person is good and that Christ is in each; it seems to have sunk into my feelings and thus I believe it now. I look forward to serving and eagerly anticipate it as a holy act and awesome privilege. I have acquired deep respect for the people I serve so simply.

Personally I feel that it has helped me spiritually as well in three ways. First, I am beginning to be aware that the community you worship with is important, that in the celebration of the liturgy you are not worshiping alone and privately. I knew this also, but now I believe it. Second, there were some personal, not good living habits that I was battling with. Now they are completely eliminated from my life and life style. Third, a rather joyful result is the fact that many people in the parish have introduced themselves to me, speaking to me in stores and other places (sometimes it takes a few minutes to realize how they know me). I feel more a part of the parish, welcome and not alone.

ACCOUNTANT AND AUDITOR

Distributing the Lord to one's wife and family at the start can be an overwhelming experience. Don, a government tax accountant and parish auditor, describes that and another moving event in his ministry.

I was surprised at my selection to be a minister of Communion, and although the option to refuse was available, I knew I would not decline. I felt that I was being called not by man but by God to perform a small but important duty previously reserved for the priest. It was a special privilege for me, since I was always taught that the host was to be looked at but touched only by the priest.

There seems to be a closer relationship to the Lord and the people of the parish as a representative of the Lord during the Mass. This closeness becomes apparent when I hold the body of Christ and distribute that same body to the people.

There were two specific instances when this nearness to the Lord was especially felt. The initial occasion was when my children first received Communion from me and I saw the tears in my wife's eyes when I lifted the host and said "The Body of Christ." The other situation was a Mass in which the congregation had the opportunity to receive under both species. As a minister of the cup for the first time, I felt, as I gazed into the cup, his nearness in a way that is beyond description. It was as if I could reach out and actually touch his face.

Every Sunday I pray that I may be worthy to receive and distribute the host in a proper manner so that when the day of judgment arrives, the Lord will consider me worthy to enter his kingdom, and say to me: "Enter my kingdom, my good and faithful servant."

MINISTER TO DAUGHTER

Diane, now in her mid-twenties, has been bedridden nearly all her life. Each month a priest visits the always cheerful young lady with Communion, but for the past three years her father every Sunday has brought the Lord home from Mass and offered this to his daughter.

When I come home after Mass each Sunday, Diane is in a very somber mood with her hands clasped. I give her Communion and read to her from the missalette.

One thing sure: Diane looks forward to it and so do I.

I feel good inside that I'm able to do this for Diane and our Lord.

FURNITURE SALESMAN: SPIRITUAL CONVERSION

Alex sells furniture at a local store throughout the week. Every Sunday, however, in addition to occasional duties at the altar, he receives two hosts in a small, blue, handmade plastic and cloth pocket or burse, and then takes his precious cargo to a home four blocks away from the church.

There he reads the day's scriptural texts, summarizes the priest's homily, prays with semi-invalid Stan and his confined, caring wife, Ann, distributes the Eucharist to them, and, finally, leaves a copy of the parish bulletin.

Alex never had met these two persons prior to assuming the role as minister of Communion to the sick.

I have had the privilege of being a minister of Communion for about four years. During this time of service for my church, my life has changed both spiritually and morally. This change was subtle, but I experienced a greater insight into my own moral behavior. Perhaps as a servant of Christ one tries to be more Christ-like, so as to better deserve the honor of presenting the body of Christ to my fellow Christians.

Spiritually I experienced a deeper comprehension of the Mass, being involved as a helper of Christ and enjoyed being closer to my Savior than I have ever been in my life.

These spiritual and moral experiences were brought to a higher plateau when I volunteered to be a minister of Communion to the sick.

My contact with another Christian, on a one-to-one basis, found my life heightened when I brought the body of Christ to someone who because of illness couldn't participate in the Mass and receive the Eucharist. By bringing the host every Sunday, I increased my spiritual awareness and helped another to come closer to Christ, making this service a twofold spiritual benefit.

The friendship between myself and my spiritual brother has deepened over the last year, to a point where I believe both of us can face his imminent death with a joy of Easter resurrection.

RETIRED: CROWN OF LIFE

For Georgianna, a woman past retirement age but remarkably active, her appointment as a distributor of the Eucharist has been the crowning event of a deeply spiritual life. That clearly emerges in her reflection.

As a minister of Communion, I find it isn't easy to put my feelings into words, but I'll try.

When you first asked me, I felt a surge of joy and goodness, but also of amazement.

Often I'd think of Jesus telling his disciples that he chose them, they didn't choose him, and I'd pray: Dear Jesus, choose me for something.

Now I pray that our Blessed Mother will stand beside me and everyone I communicate will be filled with awareness and love of God and have great joy.

I ask our Blessed Mother to place her hand under mine, as I hold my dear Jesus. By her hand, I have a holy place for my Lord to be.

I feel a change in myself, of great peace, as I keep repeating, "My Lord and my God, I love you."

I am grateful and filled with love as I feel my God so near.

After, I say prayers of thanksgiving for this great honor, and I offer up to God all of my humble feelings.

I wait with anticipation for the next time.

5

Prayerful Persons
of Faith and Joy

In the previous chapter, Cathy mentioned how she judged that certain bad personal living habits were inconsistent with her role as a eucharistic minister and had successfully eliminated them.

Alex spoke of an attempt to be more Christ-like after his appointment to this task.

The power company lineman who climbs light poles for a living remarked: "Being on the altar on Sunday distributing Communion to my family and friends makes me want to be more, to be someone that people can trust and look up to, to do what is right, not simply what is convenient or easy. I want to be closer to Jesus through my ministry and closer to others because of it."

HOLINESS AND HUMAN FRAILTY: JESUS, PAUL, KÜBLER-ROSS

Those desires for self-improvement and holiness which accompanied their functioning as special ministers of the Eucharist obviously deserve support and praise. They also reflect sentiments of the Fathers at the Second Vatican Council addressed to priests, but which apply with equal force to Communion distributors.

> Priestly holiness itself contributes very greatly to a fruitful fulfillment of the priestly ministry. True, the grace of God can complete the work of salvation even through unworthy ministers. Yet ordinarily God desires to manifest his wonders through those who have been made particularly docile to the impulse and guidance of the Holy Spirit. Because of their intimate union with Christ and their holiness of life, these men can say with the apostle: "It is no longer I that live, but Christ lives in me" (Galatians 2:20).[1]

Persons who espouse such idealism but struggle with human frailty can nevertheless take comfort in the example of Jesus and the words of Scripture.

Our Lord selected men whose faults have been highlighted in the Bible. Impetuous Peter boasted of his loyalty, then almost immediately under pressure denied his Master. The skeptic Thomas boldly asserted he would not believe unless he probed Christ's nail-prints and put his hands into Jesus' side. James and John, along with Peter, were asked by the Master to support him in Gethsemane when he felt deep sorrow, fear and distress. Instead, they fell asleep. "So you could not stay awake with me for even an hour?"[2]

The Lord's response to their drowsiness is really meant for all of us. "Be on guard, and pray that you may not undergo the test. The spirit is willing but nature is weak."[3]

The power of God's grace transformed these weak men, carrying them on to great sanctity and to the ultimate self-giving of martyrdom.

St. Paul speaks in similar fashion about human weakness and amazing grace. A thorn in the flesh, an angel of Satan continually attacked this apostle to keep him from pride.

> Three times I begged the Lord that this might leave me. He said to me, "My grace is enough for you, for in weakness power reaches perfection." And so I willingly boast of my weaknesses instead, that the power of Christ may rest upon me. Therefore I am content with weakness, with mistreatment, with distress, with persecutions and difficulties for the sake of Christ; for when I am powerless, it is then that I am strong.[4]

The grace of God, then, will be sufficient for ministers of Communion as it has and will be for others like Paul. Its end product, however, is not so much a reform of personal habits or a transformation of life style as the development of certain desirable inner qualities.

Dr. Elisabeth Kübler-Ross, whose writings on death and dying are world-known, observed once how important are the interior attitudes of clergy who visit the terminally ill. Their faith, or lack of it, will be detected by the deathly sick, sometimes without a word being spoken, and thus either encourage or discourage those hurting patients. In eucharistic ministers the positive interior qualities or their regrettable absence will likewise be evident to others in the worshiping community.

These dispositions, too, will thus build up or tear down the body of Christ.

We now wish to sketch a few of those desirable inner qualities in the eucharistic minister.

1. A PERSON OF FAITH

Inner faith is, of course, the essential foundation for all Catholic worship. Unless the interior eye passes through the external signs and symbols of our liturgies, looks beyond the words, actions and materials of our public prayer to a deeper reality present, and sees something beneath our sacramental rituals, then we are a deceived people practicing hollow, artificial, even magical ceremonies.

Faith enables us to pass through, look beyond and see beneath the outer shell. Through faith we recognize the presence of Christ in various ways within our liturgies.

Those many presences of the Lord, originally outlined so clearly in paragraph 7 of Vatican II's *Constitution on the Sacred Liturgy*, are nicely summarized in the introduction to the ritual for *Holy Communion Outside of Mass:*

> In the celebration of Mass the chief ways in which Christ is present in his Church gradually become clear. First he is present in the very assembly of the faithful, gathered together in his name; next he is present in his word, when the Scriptures are read in the Church and explained; then in the person of the minister; finally and above all, in the eucharistic sacrament. In a way that is completely unique, the whole and entire Christ, God and man, is substantially and permanently present in the sacrament. This presence of Christ under the appearance of bread and wine "is called real, not to exclude other kinds of presence as if they were not real, but because it is real *par excellence.*"[5]

An awareness of those presences and faith in them will affect the way a minister of Communion fulfills his

49

or her function. That personal faith will overflow into one's attitudes and actions.

FAITH

A change takes place within us when we become conscious that Jesus dwells in our midst as we pray together. We listen more attentively and prepare more carefully when we reflect that it is the Lord who speaks in the Scriptures. We touch, consume and handle more reverently the consecrated species when we fully appreciate that it is truly Christ's body and blood beneath the bread and wine.

Faith in this real eucharistic presence is the most critical quality for a minister of Communion. To believe that "the Holy Eucharist contains the entire spiritual treasure of the Church, that is, Christ himself, our passover and living bread";[6] to believe that "Christ the Lord is offered in the Sacrifice of the Mass when he becomes present sacramentally as the spiritual food of the faithful under the appearance of bread and wine"; to believe that "once the sacrifice is offered and while the Eucharist is reserved in churches and oratories, he is truly Emmanuel, 'God with us' "; to believe that "he is in our midst day and night; full of grace and truth, he dwells among us"—[7] to believe those truths of the Church in the depths of our hearts constitutes the "one thing only required" by the Lord for a suitable distributor of the Eucharist.[8]

That faith, however, is not a static quality. It can grow and, alas, may weaken and even be lost.

For that reason "Christians gather at Mass that they may hear and express their faith again in this assembly and, by expressing it, renew and deepen it."[9]

"People in love make signs of love, not only to express their love but also to deepen it. Love never expressed dies. Christians' love for Christ and each other, Christians' faith in Christ and in each other, must be expressed in the signs and symbols of celebration or it will die."[10]

"Faith grows when it is well expressed in celebration. Good celebrations foster and nourish faith. Poor celebrations weaken and destroy faith."[11]

The eucharistic minister, then, like the priest or deacon celebrant, can foster and nourish or weaken and destroy faith. That distributor's own inner faith is the key factor here. The following words of our American bishops about the celebrant apply as well to the minister of Communion.

"No other single factor affects the liturgy as much as the attitude, style and bearing of the celebrant: his sincere faith and warmth as he welcomes the worshiping community; his human naturalness combined with dignity and seriousness as he breaks the bread of word and Eucharist."[12]

A great opportunity, a great challenge, a great responsibility.

2. A PRAYERFUL PERSON

Out of faith develops an attitude of prayerfulness. We stand before God in a spirit of awe, reverence, and dependence.

When Moses came to Horeb, the mountain of God, an angel of the Lord appeared to him out of a bush which, though on fire, was not consumed.

As Moses moved over more closely to examine this remarkable phenomenon, God called out and said:

"Come no nearer! Remove the sandals from your

feet, for the place where you stand is holy ground. I am the God of your father," he continued, "the God of Abraham, the God of Isaac, the God of Jacob."

Moses was so shaken by all this that he hid his face, for the Jewish leader feared looking at God.[13]

That kind of "remove your sandals and hide your face" awe before our transcendent, majestic Lord will come across to people. Such an inner spirit of reverence and prayerfulness is transparent. People sense and recognize it, just as they intuit and detect its absence.

Such an attitude will affect the way we walk about the sanctuary, fold our hands, genuflect, distribute the host and hand over the cup. There should be no casualness, no rush. Rather, there should be careful, deliberate gestures, although natural and honest ones.

Dealing the particle to others as if this is a fast card game and placing the sacred bread on the tongue before a communicant can whisper "Amen" are bad habits caused rather easily by routine, but they communicate to others a lack of prayerfulness in the minister.

ADORATION

Closely akin to that spirit of prayer is the stance of adoration. The Church insists that "all the faithful show this holy sacrament the veneration and adoration which is due to God himself. . . . Nor is the sacrament to be less the object of adoration because it was instituted by Christ the Lord to be received as food."[14]

That sense of adoration expresses itself often during the eucharistic liturgy. For example, in the Gloria of the Mass the congregation shouts, as it were, "We worship you, we give you thanks, we praise you for your glory." The people's response to the Preface, as another illustration, reflects an Old Testament angelic hymn of adoration: "Holy, holy, holy Lord, God of power and might. . . ."

A spirit of prayerful adoration should permeate ministers throughout the celebration of Mass and during the distribution of the Eucharist. But it also ought to bring them frequently to the tabernacle for private, personal meditation outside of Mass. Prayer before the Lord reserved in that location finds its origin in the Mass and leads people back to the eucharistic sacrifice itself. Logically speaking, those with the greatest devotion to the Mass will at the same time have an intense relationship with Christ the Lord in the tabernacle; conversely, the person who prays regularly before the reserved sacrament should possess a deep love for holy Mass.

The Roman document on *Holy Communion Outside of Mass* addresses this matter at length:

When the faithful honor Christ present in the sacrament, they should remember that this presence is derived from the sacrifice and is directed toward sacramental and spiritual Communion.

The same piety which moves the faithful to eucharistic adoration attracts them to a deeper participation in the paschal mystery. It makes them respond gratefully to the gifts of Christ who by his humanity continues to pour divine life upon the members of his body. Living with Christ the Lord, they achieve a close familiarity with him and in his presence pour out their hearts for themselves and for those dear to them; they pray for peace and for the salvation of the world. Offering their entire lives with Christ to the Father in the Holy Spirit, they draw from this wondrous exchange an increase of faith, hope and love. Thus they nourish the proper disposition to celebrate the memorial of the Lord as devoutly as possible and to receive frequently the bread given to us by the Father.

The faithful should make every effort to worship

Christ the Lord in the sacrament, depending upon the circumstances of their own life. Pastors should encourage them in this by example and word.

Prayer before Christ the Lord sacramentally present extends the union with Christ which the faithful have reached in Communion. It renews the covenant which in turn moves them to maintain in their lives what they have received by faith and by sacraments. They should try to lead their whole lives with the strength derived from the heavenly food, as they share in the depth and resurrection of the Lord. Everyone should be concerned with good deeds and with pleasing God so that he or she may imbue the world with the Christian spirit and be a witness of Christ in the midst of human society.[15]

After the faithful and the minister have participated in the Eucharist, the Church recommends that each one who has been refreshed by Communion should remain in prayer for a period of time. That prayerful personal thanksgiving simply continues what the Mass itself does so perfectly—giving thanks to the Father through Christ and in the Spirit.[16]

Leaving the altar and the church does not mean abandoning the presence of Christ there or removing his influence on our daily work and world. "The union with Christ, to which the sacrament is directed, should be extended to the whole of Christian life. Thus the faithful, constantly reflecting upon the gift they have received, should carry on their daily work with thanksgiving, under the guidance of the Holy Spirit, and should bring forth fruits of rich charity."[17]

The rubrics for Mass mention that a priest at the Eucharist "should serve God and the people with dignity and humility. By his actions and proclamations of the word he should impress upon the faithful the living presence of God."[18]

With adaptations, that exhortation applies to eucharistic ministers who must serve with dignity and humility, impressing upon others the living presence of God. Only a prayerful person can do that.

3. A PERSON OF JOY

The presence of Jesus brought joy to people's hearts.

At the first Christmas, an angel reassured frightened shepherds with these words: "You have nothing to fear! I come to proclaim good news to you—tidings of great joy to be shared by the whole people."[19]

After his death, the risen Lord appeared to the eleven and said, "Touch me." He showed them his hands and his feet, but they were "still incredulous for sheer joy and wonder" over his presence in their midst.[20]

Following Pentecost, the first Christians lived a communal life. "They went to the temple area every day, while in their homes they broke bread. With exultant and sincere hearts they took their meals in common, praising God and winning the approval of all people."[21] There are fairly good reasons for arguing that this paragraph from the Acts of the Apostles includes an indirect reference to the Eucharist. In any event, their inner selves experienced great joy during those days together as they broke bread.

St. Paul, writing to the early believers of Galatia, taught that the fruit of the spirit is love, joy, peace, patient endurance, kindness, generosity, faith, mildness and chastity.[22]

To the Thessalonians, he simply gave this directive: "Rejoice always."[23]

The minister of Communion should experience and radiate some of that joy. He or she has indeed heard the tidings of great joy, touched the risen Jesus' body, broken bread with others at the Lord's table, received the Holy Spirit in baptism-confirmation, and accepted the mandate or encouragement of Paul to rejoice always.

Those inner qualities of peace, love and joy will, like faith and prayerfulness, be evident to parishioners. Persons with such transparent joy naturally attract others to themselves and win these people over. Their own joy is contagious; it spreads; it quietly seeps into a neighbor's being and begins to lift up that individual's spirit; it is shared without any loss to the sharer.

Having said all these things, we need to offer the eucharistic ministers a few comments about this desirable joy in connection with their feelings, their sinfulness and their approach to liturgical laws.

EMOTIONAL RESPONSE

First, with regard to joy and feelings, a Communion minister, like all those with special ministerial functions or even like every believer for that matter, needs to beware of confusing or identifying the spiritual joy we are discussing with pure feelings of elation.

They may be the same at times, but not always, or necessarily.

We can experience a profound inner serenity and yet feel blue, bad or bored. On the other hand, an individual may feel sky "high" or wildly excited and still lack deep peace and joy.

The problems which accompany routine affect every area of life, including such sacred and sublime activities as offering Mass or distributing the Eucharist. We may feel no enthusiasm, seem to take the privilege for granted and wonder if our faith has grown weak or our reverence for the sacrament has diminished.

The emotional zeal of a newly ordained priest or a

freshly installed eucharistic minister does not last forever. No one lives a life of peaks and plateaus alone; there are valleys of darkness and low moments for all.

A faith-filled celebration may be feeling-less; a feeling-filled liturgy could be faithless. So, too, a joy-filled service may appear to lose feeling, and feeling-filled worship could seem to be devoid of spiritual joy and tranquillity.

Our American bishops summarized this rather well:

> Celebrations need not fail, even on a particular Sunday when our feelings do not match the invitation of Christ and his Church to worship. Faith does not always permeate our failings. But the sign and symbols of worship can give bodily expression to faith as we celebrate. Our own faith is stimulated. We become one with others whose faith is similarly expressed. We rise above our own feelings to respond to God in prayer.[24]

Practically speaking, this means performing our task with faith, prayerfulness and care regardless of the current mood or feeling. The spirit of Christian joy and peace within us will still shine through despite what our emotions may seem to tell us at that moment.

Second, with regard to joy and our sinfulness, a bumper sticker I saw recently announced: "Christians are not saints, just saved."

That motto carries considerable wisdom with it. The basic reason for our inner joy is a realization that we have been forgiven by the blood of Christ, that salvation is possible for us because of the Lord's coming, dying, and rising. God calls us to believe in the Savior and to mirror Jesus' life in our own. But we are saved by grace, not merely by our own works.

A realization of this can bring great peace and deep

joy in the midst of our weaknesses and failures. In earlier paragraphs we have outlined the call for holiness and the model Christian behavior expected in a eucharistic minister. Those ideals remain intact. But what of lapses, sins and mistakes? These certainly cause sadness within. Should they likewise keep us from our ministry at the altar?

DISPOSITIONS FOR EUCHARISTIC SERVICE

The Church deals with that situation in some detail when it discusses the dispositions needed for Communion and, consequently, for a Communion minister.

The Eucharist continuously makes present among men the paschal mystery of Christ. It is the source of every grace and of the forgiveness of sins. Nevertheless, those who intend to receive the body of the Lord must approach it with a pure conscience and proper dispositions of soul if they are to receive the effects of the paschal sacrament.

On this account the Church prescribes "that no one conscious of mortal sin, even though he seems to be contrite, may go to the Holy Eucharist without previous sacramental confession." In urgent necessity and if no confessor is available, he should simply make an act of perfect contrition with the intention of confessing individually, at the proper time, the mortal sins which he cannot confess at present.

It is desirable that those who receive Communion daily or very often go to the sacrament of penance at regular intervals, depending on their circumstances.

Besides this, the faithful should look upon the Eucharist as an antidote which frees them from daily faults and keeps them from mortal sins; they should also understand the proper way to use the penitential parts of the liturgy, especially at Mass.[25]

58

Part of that cleansing, disposition building process involves fasting from food and drink beforehand. As a sort of review for ministers of the Eucharist, we reprint the contemporary legislation here.

Communicants are not to receive the sacrament unless they have fasted for one hour from solid food and beverages, with the exception of water.

The period of the eucharistic fast, that is, abstinence from food or alcoholic drink, is reduced to about a quarter of an hour for:

(1) the sick who are living in hospitals or at home, even if they are not confined to bed;

(2) the faithful of advanced age, even if not bedridden, whether they are confined to their homes because of old age or live in a nursing home;

(3) sick priests, even if not bedridden, or elderly priests, whether they are to celebrate Mass or to receive Communion;

(4) persons who care for the sick or aged, and the family of the sick or aged, who wish to receive Communion with them, when they cannot conveniently observe the fast of one hour.[26]

LOOK BEYOND WORD AND DEED

Third, with regard to joy and our attitude toward liturgical laws, it is difficult to be joyful or to radiate joy when we feel uptight or are preoccupied with rubrical rules and regulations. Our attention then focuses on the external deed or word and loses sight of the divine reality beneath and beyond those signs or symbols.

A few of the personal testimonies in an earlier chapter mentioned inner nervousness, worried concern, shaking hands, and moist palms as these people prepared for or discharged their ministry. A bit of that could be traced to the newness of this task and the understandable desire to perform it properly. But much of that anxiety may grow out of an excessive attention to the right procedure and undue concentration on suitable reverence.

REVERENT AND RELAXED

Here is a thumb rule for eucharistic ministers, an overall approach or attitude: "Be reverent, but relaxed; comfortable, but not casual."

The Church always urges a balanced view, a middle road in doctrinal teaching and pastoral practice. The principle we have just enunciated fits into that category.

Our bishops in the United States have only these words about the proper decorum for a eucharistic distributor. "It is of the greatest importance that the minister avoid all rush and haste. His ministration of Communion should be done with dignity and reverence."[27]

Dignity and reverence. No rush or haste. Careful. Relaxed. At ease. Natural. Oneself.

After all, the Mass, as well as other forms of liturgy, is a celebration. The initial chapter of the General Instruction for the Order of Mass carries the title, "Importance and Dignity of the Eucharistic Celebration." That brief section alone uses the term "celebration" nine times.[28] Now a celebration, however described or defined, implies a relaxed, easy, joyful event.

The Eucharist, moreover, is a paschal meal or sacred banquet in which participants eat and drink. Only on the most formal of circumstances or the very first occasion with a family or the initial dinner out with a date do we feel uptight and anxious while eating. Even in those circumstances that tension should and generally does ease after the beginning moments. It ought to be the same with us during Communion.

Rubrics for the Communion song at Mass indicate that this music "expresses the spiritual union of the communicants who join their voices in a single song, shows the joy of all, and makes the Communion procession an act of brotherhood."[29]

Such spiritual union, joy and brotherhood presumes that the participants, including the eucharistic ministers, are relaxed, while still reverent, comfortable and at ease, even though not casual or careless.

To grasp and develop these inner qualities as well as to master the mechanics of distributing Communion presupposes some parish preparation or formation program. That will be the topic of our next chapter.

6

A Parish Formation Program

A few decades ago East Syracuse, New York was, above all else, a railroad town. The old New York Central had a massive classification yard next to this community and huge steam locomotives belched black smoke as they pulled their heavy loads onto the main line west toward Buffalo or east to Albany and on branch lines north to Canada or south to Pennsylvania.

I have no hard statistics, but many of those railroad employees were certainly Catholic and their deep faith led them to build an imposing granite church a block or two from the tracks.

The New York Central is now Conrail; the steam locomotives have been replaced by quieter, cleaner diesels; the yard is smaller and works by computers; the trains are fewer, but longer; the village itself is presently more a sprawling suburb of Syracuse than a well-known railroad village.

St. Matthew's Church, however, still stands and draws crowds for its two Saturday night Masses and five

Sunday morning liturgies. Moreover, the schedule of Eucharists even reads like a railroad timetable: 5:00 and 7:15 (Saturday); 7:00; 8:15; 9:25; 10:45; 12:00 (Sunday).

In the spring of 1979, one of the associate priests at St. Matthew's was reassigned by the bishop. Because of the clergy shortage, the diocese's chief shepherd gave no assurance that a replacement would be forthcoming. To deal with this situation, the parish leadership people considered and later endorsed the notion of introducing lay or special ministers of Communion, particularly at the more crowded weekend Masses.

The urgency of that circumstance caused the staff to move a bit faster than might be ideal in terms of preparing the people and the candidates for this new development. But within two months—May to June—they were able to instruct the community, obtain fourteen potential ministers—seven men, seven women—and train these eucharistic distributors.

FORMATION OF EUCHARISTIC MINISTERS

Paragraphs in the bulletin and words from the pulpit informed the congregation about the why, who, how and when. A single three-hour evening session prepared the ministers. The formal commissioning service, repeated at each of the weekend Masses in which the Communion ministers were to be used, linked all of this together.

That formation evening began with a paraliturgical service in one of the church meeting rooms. The burning paschal candle was placed in the center of the area, lights were dimmed, one of the priests prayed using Ephesians 3:14–21 as his text, and all listened to a tape of the familiar folk song, "Be Not Afraid."

An associate pastor then welcomed the fourteen candidates and, using the "Be Not Afraid" motif, spoke about the difficulties of a beginning, the radical step this was for St. Matthew's and the staff's gratitude for their willingness to accept such a challenge.

He then outlined the evening's program and discussed the universal Church's support for what they were about in the East Syracuse parish. His explanation started with the legislation of St. Pius X concerning frequent and early Communion and concluded with Pope Paul VI's instruction *Immensae Caritatis.*

VISION OF SHARED MINISTRY

The pastor followed and described the selection process (parish council and professional staff combined to make the choices with the suggestion of names from parishioners publicly welcomed). He also offered a vision of his desires for shared ministries in St. Matthew's and the kind of community they hope that church will become.

The other associate pastor concluded this forty-five-minute introduction and overview orientation with some thoughts on the spiritual dimensions of the Eucharist.

For the second segment of the evening, participants viewed "Do This in Memory of Me," a filmstrip produced by ROA Films, Milwaukee, Wisconsin. That audio-visual examines the entire Mass and thus put into context and proper perspective the ministry which these women and men were soon to begin.

A wine and cheese break gave members of the group an opportunity to mix informally and also to note on two large newsprint sheets fixed to the wall their name, the Mass they usually attend and ones virtually impossible for them. In addition, they were challenged to come to two Masses during the ensuing weekend for a commissioning ceremony. All agreed, and thus seven were formally designated at each of the Masses within which special ministers would be distributing Communion.

After the break, one of the associates spent a lengthy period on such practicalities as what to wear, when to come up, and how to hold the ciborium. Moreover, he described the procedure when a particle is dropped ("There are droppers, snappers and snatchers at every Mass"). He also urged them not to rush and to look at the communicant. Finally, with the Last Supper words "took, blessed, broke, gave" as a framework the young priest supplied some motivational concepts for their task.

PRAYER AND PRACTICE

The group then moved upstairs to the church proper for a prayer service prepared by a priest in residence at St. Matthew's who has special musical gifts. This included recitation of the Our Father, a reading, silent meditation and singing of "O Bread of Life" to the melody and organ accompaniment of "O Salutaris Hostia," a second reading, silent meditation and listening to the song, "For I Shall See You Again," a lengthy prayer for grace-filled ministries offered in unison by the candidates, a blessing by the pastor and, finally, the singing of "God's Blessing Sends Us Forth."

Following this service, the priests spent some time with the candidates in a learning-by-doing exercise. The ministers became familiar with their proper locations in the sanctuary and nave, distributed unconsecrated hosts to each other and practiced the actions which they would be performing that next weekend.

This meeting was a full 7:00–10:30 session, but it provided the fourteen ministers with proper understanding, spiritual motivation, and practical know-how for their sacred task. The parish leaders plan to conduct renewal evenings for the eucharistic distributors a few times throughout the year to deepen their awareness and renew their enthusiasm.

The single night preparation program at St. Matthew's in East Syracuse is an illustration of what can be done on the parish level to prepare eucharistic ministers.

Here are a few additional suggestions:

• As we proposed and exemplified in Chapter 4, some exchange on the part of rookie and veteran ministers can be inspirational and supportive. A warm and encouraging invitation by the formation leader for them to share how they felt when first asked to serve or actually fulfilled this function will probably result in the kind of impressive remarks illustrated in those written responses. Such sharings are even more powerful when uttered in person than when put down on paper.

• At the initial meeting I would recommend that the ministers elect a leader or coordinator whose main task will be to arrange the schedule. This will not require a vast amount of time, but it does remove a responsibility from the priest or deacon which more properly can and should be accomplished by lay persons. Moreover, on special occasions when ministers are required (Thanksgiving, Christmas), one phone call to the coordinators resolves that need.

• Should there be terms for the ministers? I have mixed judgments about this question. On balance, however, my preference would be to make this a somewhat permanent appointment, but with a regular opportunity, for those who wish, to retire gracefully after a period of service. There are, nevertheless, arguments with merit which urge terms and a turnover of ministers.

• A diocesan or regional convocation of ministers on

an annual or semi-annual basis could prove helpful as a renewal day or evening. An outside speaker or speakers will have special effectiveness with any group, the very gathering of considerable numbers carries its own impact, and the exchange between ministers from various parishes gives mutual support.

Moreover, part of that session might be a breakdown into parish units for some discussion and practice. Thus, the parish leadership people achieve a double purpose: they offer a desirable retreat/renewal experience for their eucharistic ministers and, at the same occasion, have the opportunity for a meeting with them to discuss local details.

Finally, the presence of the bishop or his delegate for a talk, prayer service, Mass, or message reminds the ministers of the dignity, importance and wider dimension connected with their office.

RESOURCES

Religious education resource centers in the diocese or area normally have for rent some films and filmstrips suitable for the preparation session.

In addition to the ROA filmstrip noted above, planners might check into these productions which have been tested in practice and found useful.

Worshipping Wilma: a Teleketics filmstrip attempts in a concise, light-hearted, enjoyable way to offer some historical background to the Eucharist.

Eucharist: a ten minute, powerful, award-winning Teleketics film relates the Eucharist to contemporary life through a moving interplay of symbols and sights. This serves as an excellent stimulus for discussion.

Understanding the Liturgy: The fourth filmstrip of

this Alpha series covers the history of the Mass from the fourth century through the Second Vatican Council. It cleverly points out the change in our worship patterns and will show to the ministers how both their position and current practices have roots in the past.

The Bread of Life

The most frequent need for a eucharistic minister will be on *weekends, holydays* and *special occasions* at which the large congregation and many communicants together with the absence of sufficient priests or deacons could mean an undue delay in the celebration.

● Here are some practical suggestions for this situation:

1. Enough ministers should be appointed so that each person will have some respite from the task. Thus, a schedule might call for service every other or third Sunday, or each Sunday for a month with the next month off, etc.

2. At the formation session, the ministers could elect one of their members as director whose main task is to design and distribute a schedule for the future.

3. This assignment list should include the name, address and phone number of each minister, cover as much

as six months, and provide each person with the option of making switches as necessary. These individual shifts ought to be worked out with each other and not fall upon the director.

4. It may prove helpful, especially at the beginning, to publish the names of the ministers scheduled to distribute that weekend in the bulletin as a means of building community. People in the parish thus will come to know the identity of these persons who are serving them.

• *During the week* and in *other unique situations,* it may be necessary to appoint a person for a *single occasion alone.*

If the priest celebrant has the authority from his bishop to do so, he should select that person and prepare the individual before Mass begins.[1] The Roman document bestows upon the local bishop the faculty to permit individual priests exercising their sacred office to appoint a qualified person to distribute Holy Communion on a specific occasion, in case of genuine need.[2] Given the frequent occasions this can develop in the United States, a bishop might do well to extend such an authorization to all the priests of his diocese.

The person so chosen should, after the Lamb of God, be formally appointed and blessed by the celebrant according to the official rite printed at the end of Chapter 3 in this volume.[3]

• Should there be some *identification garb or symbol* for eucharistic ministers?

The United States Bishops' Committee on the Liturgy responds to that question in this fashion: "Special ministers do not wear the liturgical garb of an ordained deacon or priest, but they should be dressed neatly in a way consonant with the dignity of their functional role (e.g., coat and tie for a layman). Local usage should be followed in this matter.[4]

Some parishes have provided their ministers with a uniform sport jacket or coat. A few dioceses supply specially designed and crafted medals or pendants for the Communion distributors to denote their position. Other parishes prefer that nothing be used at all in this way. One can make a good case for either procedure—identification clothes and symbols or no such identifying measures.

• Should eucharistic ministers have a special *place,* presumably in the sanctuary?

The bishops addressed that question in 1973.

> The liturgical role of the special ministers should not be visibly confused with the distinct roles of others such as the deacon, leader of song, reader or acolyte. Special ministers should not assist the priest at the altar during Mass in the manner of a deacon. They should have an assigned place, however, and they may enter in procession with the priest, reader, servers, etc.[5]

Since then, however, permission has been extended for the distribution of Communion from the cup on Sundays. Such an introduction in the parish requires the addition of many more eucharistic ministers, and their presence in the sanctuary or nearby can cause confusion and real cluttering. It may now be the time to adjust this procedure and have the distributors remain with the congregation until the Lamb of God and then come forward.

• Does the minister *wash* his or her *hands* before and after Communion?

The rubrics say nothing about Communion distributors doing this beforehand. Common sense obviously dictates that the ministers come to church with relatively clean hands. The issue here is a ritual washing which symbolizes an inner purification similar to the priest's gesture at the preparation of gifts: "Lord, wash away my iniquity; cleanse me from my sin."

Some parishes do provide a separate basin nearby, but apart from the sanctuary where the ministers wash their hands during the Lamb of God; however, this appears to be a purely optional matter.

Various rubrics mention the minister washing his or her hands after Communion, but sometimes this appears as a directive, at others as an option.

In the *Rite for Administration of Communion by a Special Minister,* the rubric states: "After Communion, the minister washes his hands and then returns to his place."[6]

The *Rite of Distributing Holy Communion Outside of Mass with the Celebration of the Word* makes this optional. "After Communion the minister puts any particle left on the plate in the pyx, and he may wash his hands."[7]

An older version for the distribution of Communion to the sick mentions: "After Communion has been distributed, the minister purifies his hands if needed. . . ."[8] A newer text makes no mention of this washing at all.[9]

With those kind of differences in rubrical directions, it would seem that the washing of a minister's hands before or after Communion is a matter which could be left to the option of the local community.

• When does the eucharistic minister *genuflect* in the sanctuary?

The specific genuflections will depend upon the detailed arrangements for distribution at a given celebration in each parish. However, the general principles are these:

A genuflection is made immediately after opening the tabernacle door and immediately before closing it when distribution of Communion has been completed.

A genuflection is made to the Lord present on the altar before picking up the vessel with consecrated particles and after leaving the same vessel on the altar when finished.

• Does the minister *look* at the *consecrated bread or* the *communicant* when offering the Eucharist?

There is no clear-cut answer to that question. However, our actions at worship should be authentic, with the deeds we do matching the companion words we pronounce.

Older rubrics read: "In giving Communion during Mass, the minister takes a host for each communicant, raises it a little, and shows it, saying: 'The body of Christ.' The communicant answers: 'Amen.' "[10]

In effect, the minister invites each communicant to make an act of faith in the Lord present under the sign of bread. The guidelines from our American bishops even insist that the minister give the consecrated particle to a person "only after the communicant has responded 'Amen.' "[11]

Our words, then, are directed partially to the "body of Christ" as a declaration and partially to the communicant as an invitation. It would seem, therefore, that we attempt to look at both during the brief exchange: at the particle as we pronounce "The body of Christ" and at the communicant as we await the response.

More critical to the effectiveness of this rite is a sufficient pause and leisurely pace which will allow a communicant to utter the "Amen." My own experience in many churches indicates that we have already begun to slip into bad, rushed habits—distributors and communicants alike. Ministers pronounce "The body of Christ" before lifting up the particle or hand it over before the communicant has an opportunity to offer the response. Communicants, probably because of previous rushed experiences or simple nervousness, tend to speak the "Amen" before the minister can even say a word.

Some clergy find pronouncing a communicant's name during the distribution a most powerful pastoral practice. There are, of course, liabilities in this procedure—making mistakes, forgetting the name or not knowing the person. On balance, nevertheless, the spiritual benefits seem to outweigh any potential negative effects.

As the special minister becomes more comfortable with his or her ministry and the people, that option might be considered.

- The *minister normally* should *receive Communion and under both kinds.*

This suggestion simply flows from all that has been said before about the inner qualities of the minister and what will follow in the next section about Communion from the cup.

- Ministers do *not replace, only assist* the *priests.*

In the words of our bishops, "It is not envisioned that the extraordinary minister become a substitute for priests so as to free them for other duties or more leisure time."[12] Sunday Mass and Communion are the only occasions when most Catholics see their parish priest and have some personal contact with him. For the clergy to remain in the rectory or sacristy or wherever at those moments because special ministers are available would be a step backward for that community.

The specific procedure to be followed for Communion during Mass will need to be worked out in a particular parish or worshiping community. Nevertheless, it may prove useful for initial study purposes to print the rite of commissioning a special minister to distribute Holy Communion on a single occasion.

RITE OF COMMISSIONING
A SPECIAL MINISTER
TO DISTRIBUTE HOLY COMMUNION
ON A SINGLE OCCASION

10. A person who, in a case of real necessity, is authorized to distribute holy communion on a single occasion should normally be commissioned according to the following rite.

11. During the breaking of the bread and the commingling, the person who is to distribute holy communion comes to the altar and stands before the celebrant. After the Lamb of God the priest blesses him/her with these words:

> Today you are to distribute
> the body and blood of Christ
> to your brothers and sisters.
> May the Lord bless + you, N.

> R. Amen.

12. When the priest has himself received communion in the usual way, he gives communion to the minister of the eucharist. Then he gives him/her the paten or other vessel with the hosts. They then go to give communion to the people.

RITE OF DISTRIBUTING HOLY COMMUNION BY A SPECIAL MINISTER

13. A special minister of holy communion should wear the vestments customary in the country, or clothing in keeping with this sacred ministry.

14. In distributing holy communion during Mass, the minister holds the host slightly raised and says:

The body of Christ.

The communicant answers: Amen, and receives it.

After all have received communion, the minister of the eucharist cleanses his/her fingers over the paten and, if necessary, washes them and then returns to his/her place.

15. In distributing holy communion outside Mass, the special minister is to follow the rite given in the Roman Ritual: *Holy Communion and Worship of the Eucharist outside Mass.*[13]

8

The Cup of Salvation

At the Last Supper, Jesus took bread, blessed it, broke it, and gave it to his disciples, saying, "Take this and eat it; this is my body." Then he took a cup, gave thanks, and gave it to them, saying, "All of you must drink from it, for this is my blood. . . ."[1]

HISTORICAL BACKGROUND

Those words are very familiar to us, as are the famous paintings of that Holy Thursday event.

It should be evident, then, that the meaning of Holy Communion is more clearly significed when the faithful receive under both kinds—when the members of a congregation not only eat the Lord's body, but actually drink his blood under the appearance of wine. It was because of this fuller sign value that the Church from the outset until the thirteenth century in the West (continuing on to the present in the East) consistently and commonly distributed Communion under both kinds to the laity. This was throughout those years and remains today the fullest expression and most perfect fulfillment of what our Lord said, did and directed: "Let me solemnly assure you, if you do not eat the flesh of the Son of Man and drink his blood, you have no life in you."

At the same time, the Church always gave Communion under one kind when circumstances so dictated, and it recognized this as a valid, complete, true sacrament. Thus, Christians received under the sign of bread alone when communicating at home or when the Eucharist was offered to the sick, to prisoners, or to monks living in isolation. Similarly, Communion under the appearance of wine alone for infants and the gravely ill formed a standard and accepted custom throughout this period.

Practical difficulties and poor attitudes linked to produce a change in the thirteenth and fourteenth centuries. There was, naturally, no denial, but in fact a greater affirmation of the truth that each kind, bread or wine, contained the whole Christ, present body and blood, soul and divinity, in all the fullness and power of his life, sufferings and resurrection. But the faithful, for complicated historical reasons, approached the sacraments much less frequently and, unfortunately, failed to realize that the sacrifice and sacrificial meal are one in the Mass. These doctrinal and devotional attitudes, combined with contagion in times of rampant diseases, the possibility of irreverence or spilling, the hesitation of some communicants to drink from the common cup, the large numbers at Easter and other special feasts, and the scarcity of wine in northern countries, led to a gradual abandonment of Communion under both kinds.

A reaction set in during the fourteenth century, and many reformers urged a return to the early Christian tradition. However, in doing so some maintained that Communion under the sign of bread alone was invalid, a deprivation, an incomplete and erroneous fulfillment of the Lord's teaching in John's Gospel. Roman Catholics reacted in the face of those attacks and discouraged or forbade reintroduction of the practice under such doctrinal conditions.

VATICAN II—ROMAN MISSAL—NCCB

The Second Vatican Council decreed the restoration of this practice on occasions when it would be pastorally effective and spiritually beneficial. In doing so, however, a preparatory instruction was to make clear that, according to the Catholic faith, Christ is received whole and entire in a complete sacrament even when people communicate under one kind only. They are not, in such a circumstance, deprived of any grace necessary for salvation. Moreover, the catechesis should explain that the Church has the power to make laws about the administration of the sacraments and to change those regulations as long as they do not affect the very nature of the sacrament. Those alterations are dictated solely by what contemporary circumstances indicate is necessary for the reverence due to the sacrament and the spiritual good of the faithful. Finally, the Church explicitly encourages the faithful to desire Communion under both kinds.

The revised Roman Missal specifies fourteen cases when Communion may be distributed under both kinds. Moreover, later guidelines from the Congregation for Worship empower the bishops of a country to extend this permission to other situations. The National Conference of Catholic Bishops in the United States, following those norms, in November 1970 added instances to the list already determined by Rome. These included, among others, funerals, Masses for a special family observance, days of special religious or civil significance for the people of the United States, Holy Thursday, the Easter Vigil and weekday Masses.[2]

In November 1978, the bishops of the United States voted to extend further the use of Communion under both kinds to the faithful at all Masses on Sundays and holy days of obligation. As in the other cases, this remains an option, with the decision when to offer Communion from the cup resting in the hands of the parish leadership. The individual communicant should always be insured the freedom not to drink from the chalice when a church decides to offer Communion under both species.

Practically speaking, current legislation now allows Communion from the cup on almost any occasion when it would be pastorally beneficial and can be administered with appropriate reverence.

SUPPORTIVE REASONS

No justification for Communion from the cup is truly needed other than the actual example of Jesus' at the Last Supper and his command for us to do this in memory of him. Communicating under both kinds, we actually eat his body *and* drink his blood; we take and eat, take and drink.

But there are additional reasons supportive of Communion from the chalice:

• The meal aspect of the Eucharist is more fully manifested.

• The connection between the eucharistic meal and the heavenly banquet in the Father's kingdom becomes easier to grasp. "I tell you, I will not drink this fruit of

the vine from now until the day when I drink it new
with you in my Father's reign."

• It shows more clearly how the new and eternal
covenant is ratified in the blood of the Lord. We are thus
forcefully reminded of both Old and New Testament im-
ages which speak of an agreement sealed in blood between God and man:

> This is the cup of my blood,
> the blood of the new and everlasting covenant.
> It will be shed for you and for all men
> so that sins may be forgiven.

• Communion under both kinds recalls how the
Mass has deep roots in the Passover meal, a ritual ceremony in which the drinking of wine took place at designated intervals and was accompanied by brief prayers or
explanations. "Is not the cup of blessing we bless a sharing in the blood of Christ?"

• Receiving the Eucharist under the species of wine
brings out the special, festive, joyful banquet notion of
the Mass. We celebrate in the context of a sacred meal Jesus' and our resurrection from sin and death. Bread forms
a staple item for meals in our culture; wine adds a dimension of specialness and festivity to the dinner. The psalm-
ist proclaims: "You raise grass for the cattle, and
vegetation for men's use, producing bread from the earth
and wine to gladden men's hearts...."[3]

• Drinking from the chalice unites us to him who
drank the cup of salvation and suffering.
When James and John, the sons of Zebedee, asked
our Lord for preferred, privileged spots in his kingdom,

Jesus told them, "You do not know what you are asking. Can you drink the cup I shall drink or be baptized in the same bath of pain as I?"[4]

Later on, in Gethsemane, Christ indicated by his words and example what he meant. Experiencing distress and with his heart "nearly broken in sorrow," he said to Peter and the same James and John, "Remain here and stay awake with me."

St. Matthew tells us that "he advanced a little and fell prostrate in prayer." Then Jesus pleaded: "My Father, if it is possible, let this cup pass me by. Still, let it be as you would have it, not as I."

Some moments later, our Lord reiterated: "My Father, if this cannot pass me by without my drinking it, your will be done!"[5]

• To drink from the cup reminds us we are by that action filled with the Holy Spirit.

St. Paul in his first letter to the Christians at Corinth warned the readers: "You cannot drink the cup of the Lord and also the cup of demons. You cannot partake of the table of the Lord and likewise the table of demons."[6]

Instead of being filled by evil spirits, we become in Communion filled with the Holy Spirit. Our eucharistic prayers explicitly state this.

"Grant that we, who are nourished by his body and blood, may be filled with his Holy Spirit, and become one body, one spirit in Christ."[7]

"By your Holy Spirit, gather all who share this bread and wine into the one body of Christ."[8]

A patristic writer in the early Christian centuries spoke similarly: "Christ places two things before us: the bread and the chalice; and they are his body and blood . . . by which the grace of the Holy Spirit flows to us and nourishes us so as to make us immortal and incorruptible in hope.''[9]

PRACTICAL IMPLEMENTATION

The Roman Missal's General Instruction offers several methods for receiving Communion under both kinds—from the cup, by intinction (dipping the host into the precious blood), through a tube or with a spoon. However, the common acceptance of Communion in the hand, the lack of full sign value, and practical difficulties make procedures other than directly from the chalice not desirable as normal parish procedures. Our consideration here, therefore, will center on administration of the cup.

• Once the practice has been introduced for a few weeks at a given Mass, parish leaders will be able to make a reasonably accurate determination about the amount of wine which will need to be consecrated at that particular Eucharist.

Moreover, the purchase or manufacture of a sizable flagon which easily fits into the tabernacle provides a convenient vessel for storage of the surplus from one Mass to the next.

The combination of both approaches—a fairly good estimate beforehand and an available vessel for tabernacle storage afterward when necessary—will eliminate the awkward consumption by ministers of excess amounts after Communion or Mass.

That flagon as well as the other cups or chalices may be manufactured or crafted of any non-absorbent material. The base may likewise be of any other solid and worthy material, but preferably materials which do not break or deteriorate easily. Our own hierarchy opened the way for the use of other than traditional materials (silver, gold) for sacred furnishings provided that they are suitable for liturgical use, subject to the further judgment of the local ordinary in doubtful cases.[10]

Following the principles of parishioners' maximum involvement in worship and the fullest recognition or employment of unique gifts, artists on the local scene might well be encouraged to create vessels (e.g., ceramic, wood) appropriate for this function. Those creations, however, should be quality products.

In the words of the Bishops' Committee on the Liturgy, that quality "sees the hand stamp of the artist, the honesty and care that went into an object's making, the pleasing form and color and texture. Quality means love and care in the making of something, honesty and genuineness with any materials used, and the artist's special gift in producing a harmonious whole, a well-crafted work."[11]

• The altar should remain clear of items until the preparation of gifts following the General Intercessions. At that time only a single chalice and/or large flagon ought to be placed in the center of the altar. The cups and plates for distribution are kept on a side altar away from the central focus until the Lamb of God.

> Just as in other types of celebration those objects which are central in the rite are a natural focus. When the eucharistic assembly is large, it is desirable not to have the additional plates and cups necessary for Communion on the altar. A solution is to use one large breadplate and either one large chalice or a large flagon until the breaking of the bread. At the fraction, any other chalices or plates needed are brought to the altar. While the bread is broken on sufficient plates for sharing, the ministers of the cups pour

from the flagon into the Communion chalices. The number and design of such vessels will depend on the size of the community they serve.[12]

For Sunday and other liturgies with a large number of people which necessitate many ministers of Communion, the parish leadership people will need to give considerable attention to the logistics of this action. Too many distributors around the altar will block the view of the congregation, cause confusion and actually delay the breaking of bread and the pouring of the precious blood into distribution chalices.

The Lamb of God may be repeated over and over until the division has been completed. Then the final petition "Grant us peace" is used.

While appointment as a minister of Communion entitles the individual to distribute both the sacred bread and handle the cup, one parish has worked out the practical mechanics of the fraction procedure in this way.

At the Lamb of God, the cup ministers come forward from the congregation and stand in a line near the altar. The bread ministers, who have been in the sanctuary throughout the Mass, move to the altar and quickly, but reverently, assist the celebrant (and other priests if they are present) with the division of the particles and the pouring of wine into the smaller cups. As indicated above, those added plates and cups are carried to the altar at this time.

• How many ministers of the cup are needed? A good thumb rule: Two for each minister of the consecrated bread. In the beginning, a one to one ratio may suffice. However, as parishioners more and more accept Communion from the chalice, the two to one proportion will probably be required. In my eight years of experience in a parish, including crowded Masses like Thanksgiving and Holy Thursday, I have never seen a liturgy delayed or people waiting in long lines for the cup.

Nevertheless, introduction of this practice to Sunday Mass will necessitate the appointment of many additional ministers and the development of smooth mechanical procedures.

• The ministers of bread and cup receive under both kinds from the celebrant and/or other distributors, pick up the designated vessels and move to their posts. The chalice ministers should station themselves at some distance from their companion with the consecrated particles. This avoids confusion, permits lines to form without inconvenience and allows the individual who chooses not to drink from the chalice easy freedom to return to his or her place in the congregation.

• The cup is offered to the communicant with the words "The blood of Christ," the person responding "Amen." Our earlier comments about looking at the host or the communicant apply here as well.

We might note, parenthetically, that the chalice is not to be left on the altar or passed from one communicant to another. Nor should a communicant dip the host into the chalice.

• The cup should be totally handed over to the communicant, not merely tilted by the person drinking while being held by the minister. The latter procedure may be necessary for some exceptional cases (a small child, an incapacitated person, a parent with a baby in his or her arms), but the other process has been proven in practice to be superior.

• After the communicant has sipped some of the precious blood and returned the chalice, the minister wipes the rim with the purificator, turns the cup slightly, and offers it to the next person. We hardly need to mention that these should be fresh, clean cloths for each or nearly every Mass, a requirement which means that parishes must purchase an ample supply and arrange an efficient process for their laundering.

Some medical studies have indicated that this practice plus the alcoholic content of the wine minimizes the danger of communicating germs to others. Still, those with colds or other similar illnesses would naturally tend to refrain from drinking out of the cup. An occasional bulletin reminder about these studies and this common sense caution could help allay some concerns in that regard.

• Children certainly may receive from the chalice, and some, experience shows, will make that choice. However, parents might give them the experience of drinking wine at home prior to Communion from the chalice and discuss how we use this in everyday life to mark a festive, joyous occasion or even as part of our daily food and drink.

• After finishing, the cup distributor returns the chalice to the side table or to the nearby sacristy. Depending upon the local circumstance, the surplus consecrated wine will either be consumed by the minister or poured into the flagon for storage in the tabernacle until the next Mass. Naturally, the species should not be reserved in that fashion for very long, at the most a day or two. After Mass, the cups are washed and cleaned, unless this can be done out of view in that sacristy rather swiftly following Communion.

• The ministers of the cup then return to their places.

Throughout this service of others, the distributor should reflect and radiate the qualities of prayerfulness, faith and joy we discussed at length in an earlier chapter.

Carrying the Lord
to His Sick

Alex Grimshaw had rarely if ever met Stanley Thompson prior to that first Sunday when he brought the Lord to this ailing, elderly man.

Tall and ever smiling Alex, a furniture salesman during the week, had served as a special minister of Communion for several years at Holy Family Parish in Fulton, New York when we asked for volunteers to bring the Eucharist to our shut-ins on a regular weekend basis.

The two priests visit these people each month, offering them Communion and an opportunity for the sacrament of penance, but our parish leadership people felt that we might provide even more frequent service through the use of lay persons for this role.

COMMUNION: SHUT-INS, AGED, SICK—BONDS OF LOVE

In developing the ministry, they looked to Vatican documents for support and found precisely what was needed.

In *Holy Communion Outside Mass* the Roman decree states: "Pastors should see that an opportunity to receive the Eucharist is given to the sick and aged, even though not gravely sick or in imminent danger of death, frequently and, if possible, daily, especially during the Easter season."[1]

Such daily service would in no way be feasible without the assistance of religious or lay persons.

The same text also teaches: "In fact it is proper that those who are prevented from being present at the community's celebration should be refreshed with the Eucharist. In this way they may realize that they are united not only with the Lord's sacrifice but also with the community itself and are supported by the love of their brothers and sisters."[2]

Alex and the others who volunteered to fulfill this ministry help to achieve that goal. By reading the Sunday biblical passages to the shut-ins, summarizing the homily and leaving a copy of the parish bulletin, they link these sick persons more closely to the healthy worshiping community.

RESISTANCE AND PERSUASION

Stanley resisted in the beginning. He felt content with the priest's monthly visitation and questioned the appropriateness of a lay person, particularly one he did not know, bringing the Eucharist to him. This fine, distinguished gentleman had those understandable difficulties many experience accepting special ministers of Communion and also felt a reluctance to be so vulnerable and dependent upon others, especially a stranger.

A bit of gentle firmness from the pastor persuaded Stan, and soon Alex began his faithful weekend calls.

The Syracuse diocesan liturgical commission has produced some attractive, functional, but quite inexpensive purses for this purpose. Made of a plastic covering with a linen cloth interior and pocket, they can nicely hold a few particles and cost less than fifty cents each to produce.

Alex has one of them as well as the small but dignified booklet published by our bishops: *Administration of Communion and Viaticum to the Sick by an Extraordinary Minister.*[3] That, too, is relatively inexpensive, but complete and worthy of so great a ministry.

On Saturday night or Sunday morning, having arranged by telephone the precise time with Stanley, Alex participates at Mass and during Communion receives two hosts—one for Stan and one for his wife. After the Eucharist, he takes along a copy of the missalette and drives several blocks to the Thompson residence.

There he follows the prescribed ritual, proclaims the day's readings, mentions the homily's highlights, ministers Communion, prays with them and has a brief friendly visit, leaving the weekly bulletin as he departs.

A strong bond has developed between Alex and the Thompsons, a close union described in Chapter 4.

That type of ministry has grown rapidly in the United States with various approaches to it.

One parish, for example, brings all the ministers of the Eucharist to the sick up into the sanctuary after Communion where the celebrant formally sends them off on their mission of love.

Another coordinates visits with the televised Mass for shut-ins on a local station.

Others have parish ministers who may not make their calls on Sundays or limit them to one or two people, as in Alex' case, but, instead, reach out to great numbers in a nursing home or high-rise apartment or hospital and bring the Lord to them during the week.

In special circumstances, those unable to swallow the host are given the precious blood alone. The Roman document encourages this: "It is lawful to minister Communion under the appearance of wine to those who cannot receive the consecrated bread."[4] To do this, however, will require some special vessels similar to the kits used by Episcopal clergy in their ministry to the sick.

The ordinary rite for the administration of Communion to the sick by a special minister follows, edited slightly for reasons of clarity and to be used only for study purposes. The ritual text mentioned above or some book of similar dignity should be employed for the actual celebration.

ORDINARY RITE FOR COMMUNION OF THE SICK[5]

Those who cannot receive Communion in the form of bread may receive it in the form of wine. The precious blood must be carried to the sick person in a vessel so secured as to eliminate all danger of spilling. The sacrament should be administered with due regard to the individual concerned, and the rite for giving Communion under both kinds provides a choice of methods. If all the precious blood is not consumed, the minister himself must consume it and then wash the vessel as required.

INTRODUCTORY RITE

The minister approaches the sick person and greets him and the others present in a friendly manner. He may use this greeting:

Peace to this house and to all who live in it.

Any other customary form of greeting from scripture may be used. Then he places the sacrament on the table, and all adore it.

PENITENTIAL RITE

The minister invites the sick person and those present to recall their sins and to repent of them in these words:
My brothers and sisters,
to prepare ourselves for this celebration,
let us call to mind our sins.

A pause for silent reflection follows.

All say:
I confess to almighty God,
and to you, my brothers and sisters,
that I have sinned through my own fault

They strike their breast:
in my thoughts and in my words,
in what I have done,
and in what I have failed to do;
and I ask blessed Mary, ever virgin,
all the angels and saints,
and you, my brothers and sisters,
to pray for me to the Lord our God.

The minister concludes:
>May almighty God have mercy on us,
>forgive us our sins,
>and bring us to everlasting life.

The people answer:
>Amen.

Or:

The minister invites the people to recall their sins and to repent of them in these words:
>My brothers and sisters,
>to prepare ourselves for this celebration,
>let us call to mind our sins.

A pause for silent reflection follows.

The minister says:
>Lord, we have sinned against you.

The people answer:
>Lord, have mercy.

Minister:
>Lord, show us your mercy and love.

The people answer:
>And grant us your salvation.

The minister concludes:
>May almighty God have mercy on us,
>forgive us our sins,
>and bring us to everlasting life.

The people answer:
> Amen.

Or:

The minister invites the people to recall their sins and to repent of them in these words:
> My brothers and sisters,
> to prepare ourselves for this celebration,
> let us call to mind our sins.

A pause for silent reflection follows.

The minister, or someone else, makes the following or other invocations:

Minister:
> You brought us to salvation by your paschal
>   mystery:
> Lord, have mercy.

The people answer:
> Lord, have mercy.

Minister:
> You renew us by the wonders of your passion:
> Christ, have mercy.

The people answer:
> Christ, have mercy.

Minister:
> You give us your body to make us one with
>   your Easter sacrifice:
> Lord, have mercy.

95

The people answer:
> Lord, have mercy.

The minister concludes:
> May almighty God have mercy on us,
> forgive us our sins,
> and bring us to everlasting life.

The people answer:
> Amen.

THE SHORT FORM OF THE READING OF THE WORD

A brief passage from sacred scripture may then be read by one of those present or by the minister himself.

John 6:54–58:
> He who feeds on my flesh
> and drinks my blood
> has life eternal,
> and I will raise him up on the last day.
> For my flesh is real food
> and my blood real drink.
> The man who feeds on my flesh
> and drinks my blood
> remains in me, and I in him.
> Just as the Father who has life sent me
> and I have life because of the Father,
> so that man who feeds on me
> will have life because of me.
> This is the bread that came down from heaven.
> Unlike your ancestors who ate and died
> nonetheless,
> the man who feeds on this bread shall live forever.

John 14:6:
> Jesus told him:
> "I am the way, and the truth, and the life;
> no one comes to the Father but through me."

John 14:23:
> Jesus answered:
> "Anyone who loves me
> will be true to my word,
> and my Father will love him;
> we will come to him
> and make our dwelling place with him."

John 15:4:
> Live on in me, as I do in you,
> No more than a branch can bear fruit of itself
> apart from the vine,
> can you bear fruit
> apart from me.

John 15:5:
> I am the vine, you are the branches.
> He who lives in me and I in him,
> will produce abundantly,
> for apart from me you can do nothing.

1 Corinthians 11:26:
> Every time, then, you eat this bread and
>   drink this cup,
> you proclaim the death of the Lord until
>   he comes.
> We have come to know and to believe
>   in the love God has for us.
> God is love,
> and he who abides in love

abides in God,
and God in him.

See the *Rite of Anointing and Pastoral Care of the Sick*
(nos. 247ff. or 153ff.) for a further selection of texts.
The readings for Sundays and feastdays could be used
here followed by a short summary of the homily and
even the general intercessions.

HOLY COMMUNION

The minister then introduces the Lord's Prayer in these
or similar words:
> Now let us pray together to the Father in the
> words given us by our Lord Jesus Christ.

He continues with the people:
> Our Father . . .

Then the minister shows the holy eucharist, saying:
> This is the Lamb of God
> who takes away the sins of the world.
> Happy are those who are called to his supper.

The sick person and the other communicants say once:
> Lord, I am not worthy to receive you,
> but only say the word and I shall be healed.

The minister goes to the sick person and, showing him
the sacrament, says:
> The body of Christ (or: The blood of Christ).

The sick person answers:
> Amen.

and receives communion.

Others present then receive in the usual manner.

After communion the minister washes the vessel as usual. A period of silence may now be observed.

The minister then says the concluding prayer:
> Let us pray.
> God our Father, almighty and eternal,
> we confidently call upon you,
> that the body [and blood] of Christ
> which our brother (sister) has received
> may bring him (her)
> lasting health in mind and body.
> We ask this through Christ our Lord.

The people answer:
> Amen.

Other prayers may be chosen:
> Father,
> you have brought to fulfillment the work of
>   our redemption
> through the Easter mystery of Christ your Son.
> May we who faithfully proclaim his death and
>   resurrection in these sacramental signs
> experience the constant growth of your
>   salvation in our lives.
> We ask this through Christ our Lord.

Or:

> Lord,
> you have nourished us with one bread from
>   heaven.
> Fill us with your Spirit,
> and make us one in peace and love.
> We ask this through Christ our Lord.

Or:

> Lord,
> may our sharing at this holy table make us holy.
> By the body and blood of Christ
> join all your people in brotherly love.
> We ask this through Christ our Lord.

Or:

> Father,
> you give us food from heaven.
> By our sharing in this mystery
> teach us to judge wisely the things of earth
> and to love the things of heaven.
> Grant this through Christ our Lord.

Or:

> Lord,
> we give thanks for these holy mysteries
> which bring to us here on earth
> a share in the life to come,
> through Christ our Lord.

Or:

> All-powerful God,
> you renew us with your sacraments.
> Help us to thank you by lives of faithful service.
> We ask this through Christ our Lord.

Or:

> God our Father,
> you give us a share in the one bread and
>   the one cup
> and make us one in Christ.

Help us to bring your salvation and joy
to all the world.
We ask this through Christ our Lord.

Or:

Lord,
you renew us at your table with the
     bread of life.
May this food strengthen us in love
and help us to serve you in each other.
We ask this in the name of Jesus the Lord.

Or:

Lord,
we thank you for the nourishment you give us
through your holy gift.
Pour out your Spirit upon us
and in the strength of this food from heaven
keep us single-minded in your service.
We ask this in the name of Jesus the Lord.

Or:

Lord,
we are renewed by the breaking of one bread.
Keep us in your love
and help us to live the new life Christ won for us.
Grant this in the name of Jesus the Lord.

During the Easter season the following prayers are preferred:
Lord,
you have nourished us with your Easter
     sacraments.
Fill us with your Spirit

and make us one in peace and love.
We ask this through Christ our Lord.

Or:

Lord,
may this sharing in the sacrament of your Son
free us from our old life of sin
and make us your new creation.
We ask this in the name of Jesus the Lord.

Or:

Almighty and ever-living Lord,
you restored us to life
by raising Christ from death.
Strengthen us by this Easter sacrament;
may we feel its saving power in our daily life.
We ask this through Christ our Lord.

CONCLUDING RITE

Then the minister invokes God's blessing and, crossing himself, says:

May the Lord bless us,
protect us from all evil
and bring us to everlasting life.

Or:

May the almighty and merciful God bless and
protect us,
the Father, and the Son, and the Holy Spirit.

The people answer:
Amen.

Afterward the minister could visit in a friendly way with the people and leave a copy of the parish bulletin.

SHORT RITE FOR COMMUNION OF THE SICK FOR PLACES LIKE HOSPITALS OR NURSING HOMES[6]

This shorter rite is to be used when communion is given in different rooms of the same building, such as a hospital. Elements taken from the ordinary rite may be added according to circumstances.

The rite may begin in the church or chapel or in the first room, where the minister says the following antiphon:

> How holy this feast
> in which Christ is our food:
> his passion is recalled,
> grace fills our hearts,
> and we receive a pledge of the glory to come.

Other antiphons may be chosen:

> How gracious you are, Lord:
> your gift of bread from heaven
> reveals a Father's love and brings us perfect joy.
> You fill the hungry with good things
> and send away empty the rich in their pride.

Or:

> Body of Jesus, born of the Virgin Mary,
> body bowed in agony,
> raised upon the cross
> and offered for us in sacrifice,

body pierced and flowing with blood and water,
come at the hour of our death
as our living bread,
the foretaste of eternal glory:
come, Lord Jesus,
loving and gracious Son of Mary.

Or:

I am the living bread
come down from heaven.
If anyone eats this bread
he shall live for ever.
The bread I will give is my flesh
for the life of the world.

Then the minister may be escorted by someone carrying
a candle. He says to all the sick persons in the same room
or to each communicant individually:

This is the Lamb of God
who takes away the sins of the world.
Happy are those who are called to his supper.

The one who is to receive communion then says once:

Lord, I am not worthy to receive you,
but only say the word and I shall be healed.

He receives communion in the usual manner.

The rite is concluded with a prayer which may be said in
the church or chapel or in the last room:

Let us pray.
God our Father, almighty and eternal,
we confidently call upon you,
that the body [and blood] of Christ
which our brother (sister) has received

may bring him (her)
lasting health in mind and body.
We ask this through Christ our Lord.

The people answer:
Amen.

Other prayers may be chosen from those given in the ordinary rite, nos. 210–222.

RITE FOR VIATICUM OR COMMUNION
FOR THOSE SERIOUSLY ILL OR NEAR DEATH'

When the communicant is very seriously ill or deemed near the point of death, the Church administers Communion under the form of Viaticum. This term, a derivative of the Latin original, literally translates "a journey with you"; its meaning, however, is that the eucharistic Lord will be both food, strength, comfort and companion for the dying person on his or her trip from this life to the next.

The host or sacred particle, as well as the consecrated wine if offered, is the same. However, there are different prayers and a slightly altered format.

A new minister of Communion would probably not be called upon to administer Viaticum in the very beginning days because of the pastoral sensitivities involved. Once asked to do so, however, a brief study of the Viaticum ceremony provided in the ritual for Communion to the sick we have mentioned should be sufficient. By that time the minister will be quite comfortable with the basic rite for distributing the Eucharist to the ill.

Those who are regularly involved in this ministry

for the sick might find helpful a volume by the present author, *Together by Your Side: A Book for Comforting the Sick and the Dying.*[8] It provides guidelines to assist those caring for the seriously ill and prayers or readings to be used by persons standing by those desperately sick.

10

A Priestless People

Every weekend Father Maurice Montreuil, an Oblate of Mary Immaculate, originally from Canada, but all his priestly life a missionary in the tiny African kingdom of Lesotho, climbs into a Land Rover and drives to two or three out-stations for Mass.

His simple but comfortable residence and main church is in Mafeteng, a city of ten thousand people around fifty-five miles via black top road from the capital city of Maseru. He offers the liturgy there, but also makes his way to these other communities, not over paved highways, but across bumpy, dirt paths, up and down steep inclines, and through difficult terrain accessible, vehicle-wise, only by such a sturdy, four-wheel drive machine like his Land Rover.

Father Maurice has only five of these out-stations, a relatively small number for a missionary, but obviously he cannot visit each of them every weekend. During his absence, however, Catholics of the villages under the direction of catechists or community leaders gather for prayer and worship.

In our day, people at such out-stations may remain priestless for many Sundays, but they need not be deprived of Communion on those weekends when the Oblate missionary cannot come.

Pope Paul VI in his instruction approved the appointment of qualified persons to give the Eucharist to themselves and to other members of the congregation when there is no priest, deacon or acolyte. In case of necessity, these ministers would even be designated in a permanent way.[1]

That situation certainly exists in many missionary areas like Lesotho. Throughout the United States this is clearly a much less frequent circumstance, although in outlying, rural, sparsely settled districts a roughly parallel condition may well prevail.

Nevertheless, in metropolitan settings there may be occasions in which a community of believers may wish to gather for a prayer service with Holy Communion, even though a priest cannot be present to offer Mass.

Thus, for example, during vacation periods weekday Eucharists are often canceled when one or two of the parish priests are temporarily absent. Because of work or family obligations, regular daily Massgoers may not have the option of participating at another hour or traveling to a different, neighboring church. The instruction of Paul VI and the later rite provided by this offers an alternative in those circumstances. Other members of the church staff (e.g., religious or lay parish ministers) or already designated special ministers of Communion could lead the group in prayer and distribute the Lord to them.

The ritual below suggests appropriate readings. However, the community may use instead the lectionary readings for what might otherwise be the day's Mass—either for a saint, the season or a votive observance.

In parishes where, during weekdays, the Liturgy of

the Hours is linked with the celebration of Mass, a modified form of that might also be followed. Thus, in the instance of morning or evening prayer, the psalms would replace the penitential rite, the general intercessions would be inserted after the Gospel reading or homily, and the canticle of Zechariah or Mary, with appropriate antiphon, would follow after Communion and before the concluding prayer. The General Instruction for the Liturgy of the Hours details precisely how this should be done.[2]

When a small group assembles for such a Communion service without priest or deacon, the special minister, with approval of the pastor and parish leadership people, might share a few reflections with the community and invite brief comments upon the day's readings or feast.

What follows below is the basic format from the Roman ritual for distributing Communion by a special minister with a celebration of the word. It has been edited for study purposes to fit the situation when the leader is an extraordinary minister of the Eucharist, not a priest or deacon. For an actual celebration, the ritual book itself should be employed.[3]

RITE OF DISTRIBUTING HOLY COMMUNION OUTSIDE OF MASS WITH THE CELEBRATION OF THE WORD BY A SPECIAL MINISTER

This rite is to be used chiefly when Mass is not celebrated or when communion is not distributed at scheduled times. The purpose is that the people should be nourished by the word of God. By hearing it they learn that the marvels it proclaims reach their climax in the paschal mystery of which the Mass is a sacramental memorial and in which they share by communion. Nourished by God's word, they are led on to grateful and fruitful participation in the saving mysteries.

INTRODUCTORY RITES

After the people have assembled and preparations for the service are complete, all stand for the greeting of the minister.

If the minister is not a priest or deacon, he greets those present with these or similar words:
> Brothers and sisters,
> the Lord invites us (you) to his table
> to share in the body of Christ:
> bless him for his goodness.

The people answer:
> Blessed be God for ever.

The penitential rite follows, and the minister invites the people to recall their sins and to repent of them in these words:
> My brothers and sisters,
> to prepare ourselves for this celebration,
> let us call to mind our sins.

A pause for silent reflection follows.

All say:
> I confess to almighty God,
> and to you, my brothers and sisters,
> that I have sinned through my own fault

They strike their breast:
> in my thoughts and in my words,
> in what I have done,
> and in what I have failed to do;
> and I ask blessed Mary, ever virgin,
> all the angels and saints,
> and you, my brothers and sisters,
> to pray for me to the Lord our God.

The minister concludes:
> May almighty God have mercy on us,
> forgive us our sins,
> and bring us to everlasting life.

The people answer:
> Amen.

Or:

The minister invites the people to recall their sins and to repent of them in these words:
> My brothers and sisters,
> to prepare ourselves for this celebration,
> let us call to mind our sins.

A pause for silent reflection follows.

The minister says:
> Lord, we have sinned against you.

The people answer:
> Lord, have mercy.

Minister:
> Lord, show us your mercy and love.

111

The people answer:
> And grant us your salvation.

The minister concludes:
> May almighty God have mercy on us,
> forgive us our sins,
> and bring us to everlasting life.

The people answer:
> Amen.

Or:

The minister invites the people to recall their sins and to repent of them in these words:
> My brothers and sisters,
> to prepare ourselves for this celebration,
> let us call to mind our sins.

A pause for silent reflection follows.

The minister, or someone else, makes the following or other invocations:

Minister:
> You brought us to salvation by your paschal
> mystery:
> Lord, have mercy.

The people answer:
> Lord, have mercy.

Minister:
> You renew us by the wonders of your passion:
> Christ, have mercy.

The people answer:
> Christ, have mercy.

Minister:
> You give us your body to make us one
>> with your Easter sacrifice:
> Lord, have mercy.

The people answer:
> Lord, have mercy.

The minister concludes:
> May almighty God have mercy on us,
> forgive us our sins,
> and bring us to everlasting life.

The people answer:
> Amen.

CELEBRATION OF THE WORD OF GOD

The Liturgy of the Word now takes place as at Mass. Texts are chosen for the occasion either from the Mass of the day or from the votive Masses of the Holy Eucharist or the Precious Blood, the readings from which are in the Lectionary. The Lectionary offers a wide range of readings which may be drawn upon for particular needs, such as the votive Mass of the Sacred Heart.

There may be one or more readings, the first being followed by a psalm or some other chant or by a period of silent prayer.

After the reading of the Gospel, the minister might share a few thoughts or invite brief comments from the community assembled for this celebration.

The celebration of the word ends with the general intercessions.

THE SHORT FORM OF THE READING OF THE WORD

John 6:54–55; John 6:54–58; John 14:6; John 14:23; John 15:4; 1 Corinthians 11:26; 1 John 4:16.

This form of service is used when the longer, more elaborate form is unsuitable, especially when there are only one or two for Communion and a true community celebration is impossible. Omitting the celebration of the word of God, the minister or other person should read a short scriptural text referring to the bread of life.

HOLY COMMUNION

After the prayer the minister goes to the place where the sacrament is reserved, takes the ciborium or pyx containing the body of the Lord, places it on the altar and genuflects. He then introduces the Lord's Prayer in these or similar words:

> Let us pray with confidence to the Father
> in the words our Savior gave us:

He continues with the people:

> Our Father . . .

The minister may invite the people in these or similar words:

> Let us offer each other the sign of peace.

All make an appropriate sign of peace, according to local custom.

The minister genuflects. Taking the host, he raises it

slightly over the vessel or pyx and, facing the people, says:

> This is the Lamb of God
> who takes away the sins of the world.
> Happy are those who are called to his supper.

The communicants say once:

> Lord, I am not worthy to receive you,
> but only say the word and I shall be healed.

If the minister receives communion, he says quietly:

> May the body of Christ bring me to
> everlasting life.

He reverently consumes the body of Christ.
Then he takes the vessel or pyx and goes to the communicants. He takes a host for each one, raises it slightly, and says:

> The body of Christ.

The communicant answers:

> Amen,

and receives communion.

During the distribution of communion, a hymn may be sung.

After Communion the minister puts any particle left on the plate into the pyx, and he may wash his hands. He returns any remaining hosts to the tabernacle and genuflects.

A period of silence may now be observed, or a psalm or song of praise may be sung.

115

The minister then says the concluding prayer:
Let us pray.
Lord Jesus Christ,
you gave us the Eucharist
as the memorial of your suffering and death.
May our worship of this sacrament of your
    body and blood
help us to experience the salvation you won
    for us
and the peace of the kingdom
where you live with the Father and the
    Holy Spirit,
one God, for ever and ever.

The people answer:
Amen.

Others prayers may be chosen. See the Ordinary Rite of Communion to the Sick for texts.

CONCLUDING RITE

If the minister is not a priest or a deacon, he invokes God's blessing and, crossing himself, says:
May the Lord bless us,
protect us from all evil
and bring us to everlasting life.

or

May the almighty and merciful God
bless and protect us,
the Father, and the Son, + and the Holy Spirit.

The people answer:
Amen.

Finally the minister says:
Go in the peace of Christ.

The people answer:
Thanks be to God.

Then after the customary reverence, the minister leaves.

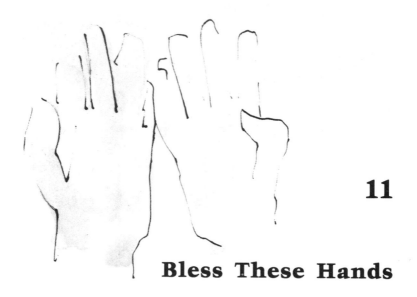

11

Bless These Hands

The Church hopes that all ministers around the altar will "serve God and the people with dignity and humility." Moreover, it desires that by their actions, they "should impress upon the faithful the living presence of Christ."[1]

A spirit of routine, however, can creep into the most sacred of actions, often blunting some of their spiritual effectiveness for both the ministers and recipients.

A moment or period of prayerful preparation prior to each occasion in which the special minister distributes the Eucharist helps to counteract that tendency. It makes us more conscious of what we are about, more aware of our important office of immense love.

IMMEDIATE PREPARATION

When the priest and other ministers assemble immediately prior to the entrance procession, a brief pause for joint prayer can settle everyone down, initiate the process of withdrawing from daily concerns and of plunging into transcendent realities, foster a spirit of quiet recollection and heighten our consciousness of the sublime mystery before us.

During that moment the priest might:

• Simply invite all the ministers to pray silently in preparation for the celebration;

• Ask, with an appropriate introduction, the assembled group to recite a common prayer like the Our Father, Hail Mary or Glory Be;

• Lead the ministers in spontaneous prayer suitable for the situation ("O God our Father, we ask you to send your Spirit in our hearts today. Help us to lead our people in worship. May we truly believe in what we do and thus inspire our community to believe as well. We ask this, Father, through Jesus Christ your Son who is present in our midst now, who will soon speak to us in the word and who comes to us in a special way at Holy Communion");

• Have a large framed copy of the prayer below or one similar on the wall and request all the ministers to pray the text together out loud;

• Use a combination of the above.

PRAYER FOR EUCHARISTIC MINISTERS[2]

Jesus, bless these hands
   you have chosen
   as your tools.

119

Jesus, always keep us aware
   and in awe
   of our sacred mission.

Jesus, make us worthy
   of this great ministry
   we have humbly accepted.

Jesus, send us out
   into the world
   to distribute your love.

REMOTE PREPARATION

Those about to be involved in any significant, serious event or experience spend time in preparation: a couple for the wedding, parents for a birth or baptism, student for an exam, musician for a concert, contractor before a bid, lecturer for some major address.

A similar, short period of preparation prior to each occasion when one is to function as a special minister of the Eucharist will, like the pause immediately before Mass or the Communion celebration, intensify our consciousness of this sublime role.

There are below five sets of such preparation periods. Each one has been designed for a three-day period before the minister's assignment on a particular Sunday, feast or occasion. The pattern is a simple one: patron saint, grace to be sought, scriptural passage, some reflection, silent period of meditation, the concluding prayer above. Obviously all types of variations and substitutions are permitted and encouraged.

These periods of preparation need not be lengthy sessions. However, fidelity to the three-day experience should bear spiritual fruit during the person's actual exercise of his or her eucharistic ministry.

SET 1: ROOTS IN THE PAST

FIRST DAY

Patron Saint: Peter. Most of us can identify well with St. Peter. His humanness is so much like ours. He spoke first, thought later; was enthusiastic, but faltered badly when times grew difficult or when he realized he was over his head; he made great promises, but failed to keep them. Peter was weak, but willing. Yet Jesus saw goodness there and entrusted his Church to him.

Grace Sought: To be conscious of our rich tradition, the ancient roots of our Church, and to deepen the loyalty to Peter and his successor which flows from such an awareness.

Scripture Reading: Matthew 16:13–20; Mark 8:27–30; Luke 9:18–21.

Reflection: The passage from St. Matthew has long been cited as the prime scriptural basis in support of the papacy. However, it would be good to read the corresponding texts as they occur in the other Gospel readings. We will follow this pattern throughout these days of preparation. A careful, reflective, comparative reading of incidents when they are recorded in several accounts will yield some surprising insights. Little details unnoticed before leap out at us.

In addition, we suggest that you have or obtain a substantial Bible containing both the Old and the New Testament as well as good footnotes. *The New American Bible,* for example, has some interesting and informative comments accompanying this passage.

In all accounts, however, note that it is Peter who responds in the name of the other apostles and disciples. Peter, their leader; Peter, our leader; Peter whose church in Rome contains a statue of the man with an outstretched foot worn smooth by the loving touch of millions over the years; Peter whose successor is our Holy Father.

Silent Period of Meditation
Prayer for Eucharistic Ministers

SECOND DAY

Patron Saint: Saints in our lives. We are not talking here about canonized saints, persons officially declared by the Church to be in heaven. Our attention is on a cluster of persons in our background who were very holy, died close to the Lord and now surely must be with God. It was their example, their teaching, and their big and little religious gestures that made us Catholics today. They handed down a heritage to us.

I can think of my own mother and her great dedication to the Church, her patience in suffering, the rosary in her hands, and her love for the Eucharist, or, of my four maiden aunts who for years went to daily Mass and prayed that my brother or I would become a priest. Outside the family, there were those good priests, teachers, and friends who shared the richness of their own faith with me.

A few moments of reflection will enable you to draw up a similar list, and on this day we ask their intercession before the Lord to help us properly fulfill our function.

Grace Sought: To be faithful to that which has been handed down to me by those contemporary saints in my life.

122

Scripture Reading: Matthew 13:53–58; Mark 6:1–6; Luke 4:16–30; John 6:41–42.

Reflection: These passages fix Jesus in a family setting—a carpenter's son and the son of Mary.

Because of the Church's faith in our Lady's perpetual virginity—she was a virgin before, during, and after the birth of Christ—the texts here have caused some difficulties on first glance in that connection.

Scholars respond to the question in this way:

a. Jesus was considered by his townsfolk and fellow citizens to be the carpenter's son, the child of Joseph. The scriptural account merely reports what was the commonly accepted fact of the day without asserting or denying the virginal conception of Christ.

b. The words "brothers" and "sisters" are translations of two terms used by Greek-speaking Jews or Semites which included not only an ordinary blood brother or sister, but also a nephew, niece, half-brother, half-sister, and cousin. Consequently, the use of the words does not necessarily mean that Mary had other children and that Jesus had blood brothers or sisters. The belief of the Church is thus not compromised by these Gospel excerpts.

In any event, our Lord did gain most of his early Jewish religious training from his parents and went down to Nazareth at the age of twelve and was obedient to them.

Silent Period of Meditation
Prayer for Eucharistic Ministers

THIRD DAY

Patron Saint: Pope St. Pius X. Our saint for this day has become famous as the Pope of first and frequent Communion. At the turn of our century that Holy Father issued a decree urging the practice by which children would receive the Eucharist as soon as they could distinguish between ordinary bread and the consecrated particles. In the decades or even centuries prior to that document, first reception of Communion was normally delayed until a later age, perhaps twelve or fourteen. Moreover, in this same text, he encouraged Catholics to approach the altar frequently, even daily. That, too, had not been a common practice in the ages before Pius X became the Vicar of Christ. As we observed earlier, he also gave strong official support for the liturgical movement and for the reform of Church music.

Grace Sought: To take advantage of the opportunity to receive the Eucharist frequently, even daily.

Scripture Reading: John 6.

Reflection: This section from St. John is the classic biblical text explaining, so to speak, the theological dimensions of the Eucharist. Ministers of Communion would do well to reread regularly and often all of that chapter. In it we see the intimate connection between Old Testament events, our Lord's life and this gift—the bread from heaven.

If you have time, you might go back to the Book of Exodus, Chapter 16, and learn about the manna in the desert, a miracle mentioned by Jesus in his preaching on the Eucharist. What happened then was a type, a prefigurement of what our Lord would do much later.

The wonderful multiplication of loaves and fishes similarly set the stage for and pointed to the later institution of Mass at the Last Supper.

In the Scripture reading we also have the incident of Christ walking on the sea, a teaching miracle which indicates how critical faith is for a follower of the Lord.

A similar faith enables us to realize that when we eat this bread and drink this wine we actually feed on Jesus' flesh and drink his blood. That food will nourish, sustain and strengthen us as it did the Israelites centuries ago.

Silent Period of Meditation
Prayer for Eucharistic Ministers

SET 2: CALLED TO GREATNESS

FIRST DAY

Patron Saint: St. John the Baptist. Our saint for today had one task: to prepare people for the coming of the Lord. Conceived by elderly parents and freed from sin in the womb of his mother by the presence of Jesus within Mary's own body, this unique child grew up, matured in the spirit and lived in the desert wilderness until he began his public preaching. A fierce looking and living figure, wearing only camel's hair and a leather belt, eating grasshoppers and wild honey, he called a spade a spade. John urged repentance for sins and conversion to a new life, pointed out Jesus to others, withdrew from the limelight when our Lord came on the scene, and died, beheaded, because he criticized the morals of a local ruler.

Grace Sought: To turn away from our selfish selves and leave our sinfulness behind.

Scripture Reading: Mark 1:1–14; Luke 3:1–22.

Reflection: If you have some extra time, read through the first two chapters of St. Luke's Gospel and note the parallels between John the Baptist and Jesus. For example, the angel visited Zechariah with a message about Elizabeth's forthcoming pregnancy, and the angel Gabriel came to Mary with a similar invitation; Mary responded to these events with a canticle of praise, and Zechariah, filled with the Holy Spirit, blessed the Lord with his own canticle after John's birth.

John called his listeners to change their lives. Jesus did the same. "Reform your lives and believe in the Gospel! This is the time of fulfillment. The reign of God is at hand!" So we read in Mark's first chapter.

That call to conversion, to greatness has a special relevance for eucharistic ministers.

Silent Period of Meditation
Prayer for Eucharistic Ministers

SECOND DAY

Patron Saint: All the apostles. As we will see below, the initial response of these men to the Lord's call was immediate and total. Later their human weakness caused them to falter or hesitate until the coming of the Holy Spirit transformed these people into courageous leaders and preachers, all ready to die for the sake of the Lord.

Grace Sought: To have confidence in the power of grace to transform us.

Scripture Reading: Matthew 4:18–22; Mark 1:16–20; Luke 5:2–11; 6:12–16.

Reflection: Reading these several brief accounts about the calling of the first disciples, one catches an enthusiasm and generosity, a total openness to whatever the Lord has in store for them.

"They immediately abandoned their nets and became his followers."

"He called them, and immediately they abandoned boat and father to follow him."

"He summoned them on the spot. They abandoned their father Zebedee, who was in the boat with the hired men, and went off in his company."

"With that they brought their boats to land, left everything, and became his followers."

126

Notice that James and John apparently came from a well-to-do fisherman's family. Zebedee had hired hands and thus was engaged in a business rather than a father simply seeking to catch enough fish for the family table.

The last passage, typical of St. Luke, offers us a portrait of Jesus as a man of deep prayer, going out to a solitary mountain spot to pray, "spending the night in communion with God." Before such an important decision, Christ set aside time to visit with the Father about it.

In your new ministry, do you feel called by the Lord in similar fashion to follow him more closely and love him more dearly?

Silent Period of Meditation
Prayer for Eucharistic Ministers

THIRD DAY

Patron Saint: Mary, the mother of Jesus and our mother. Conceived without stain and sinless in her life, our Lady was prompt in accepting the Lord's will and swift to help her aging, pregnant relative. That openness to God's plan led her to let go when Jesus began his public ministry and to offer her only Son on the cross to their Father in heaven.

Grace Sought: To imitate Mary in my ministry.

Scripture Reading: Luke 1:26–38.

Reflection: The fifteen mysteries of the rosary and the yearly celebration of Mary's feasts have made the major events of our Lady's life familiar to us.

If you have spare moments, however, you might read through these incidents involving the Blessed Mother.

127

Her visitation to Elizabeth (Luke 1:39–56).
The birth of Jesus (Luke 2:1–20).
Jesus' presentation in the temple (Luke 2:22–40).
The finding of Jesus in the temple (Luke 2:41–52).
Jesus' public comments about Mary and his family
(Mark 3:31–35).
The marriage feast of Cana (John 2:1–12).
At the foot of the cross (John 19:25–27).
After the ascension in the upstairs room preparing for Pentecost (Acts 1:12–14).
Probably alluded to in John's version (Revelation 12).

Mary was a woman of faith and trust who quickly responded "yes" when God invited her to share in a noble work and called her to something greater.

Silent Period of Meditation
Prayer for Eucharistic Ministers

SET 3: A PRAYERFUL PERSON

FIRST DAY

Patron Saint: St. Stephen. As the early Church rapidly grew, the twelve apostles recognized that they were not doing justice to the word of God or to the hurting people of their community. Thus they looked around for some helpers, for seven men who were recognized as deeply spiritual and prudent. Stephen, "a man filled with faith and the Holy Spirit," was one of those chosen.[3] The twelve prayed over them and imposed hands upon these men whom we call deacons.

Stephen, filled with grace and power, worked great wonders and signs among the people. Ultimately, however, he angered the religious leaders, was falsely accused, and then was stoned to death. Throughout the accusations, nevertheless, his face seemed like that of an angel.

Grace Sought: To forgive others and to ask others for forgiveness.

Scripture Reading: Acts 7:51–81.

Reflection: The entire story of St. Stephen, covering the sixth and seventh chapters of the Acts of the Apostles, is well worth reading.

In the concluding section about his martyrdom, we ·see the vision Stephen had of God, his prayer of abandonment (good for us before sleep at night), the desire he had to forgive those stoning onlookers, and his concern that the Lord would forgive them.

Silent Period of Meditation
Prayer for Eucharistic Ministers

SECOND DAY

Patron Saint: St. Francis of Assisi. The poor little man of Italy is probably our most popular saint in contemporary society. The relaxed, human and joyful approach of most Franciscan friars seems to reflect the image we commonly hold of St. Francis. He loved flowers and birds, the sun and the moon, spoke a message of love and peace ("Lord, make me an instrument of your peace"), and has inspired millions by his single-minded devotion to Christ.

What many overlook or do not know is the fierce penitential life Francis followed and his frequent withdrawal to an isolated, wild mountainside retreat for days of solitude and prayer.

Grace Sought: To spend some time each day in personal, private prayer.

129

Scripture Reading: Matthew 26:36–46; Mark 14:32–42; Luke 22:39–46.

Reflection: In the General Instruction for the Liturgy of the Hours, the Church gives us a beautiful picture of Jesus as a man of prayer. In articles 3–4, we read a summary of the frequent occasions in Sacred Scripture when our Lord spoke with his Father.

For example, the Savior prayed before he called the apostles, at the multiplication of the loaves, in his transfiguration on the mountain, healing the deaf mute, raising Lazarus, teaching the apostles how to pray, and blessing little children.

Moreover, he would retire into the desert or hills (St. Francis no doubt gained inspiration for this from Christ) to pray, rise early in the morning for prayer, and sometimes spend the whole night praying before a major decision or incident in his life.

Jesus also taught us how to pray and commanded us to do so.

Silent Period of Meditation
Prayer for Eucharistic Ministers

THIRD DAY

Patron Saint: Your own personal or favorite saint. Nearly every Catholic has one. It may be the holy person you were named after or simply a saint that you feel close to and comfortable with in prayer. St. Thérèse, the Little Flower? St. Anthony? St. Jude? St. Lucy? St. Rose of Lima? St. John Neumann?

Grace Sought: To call more frequently upon my favorite saint and imitate that holy person's virtues.

Scripture Reading: Matthew 17:1–9; Mark 9:2–9; Luke 9:28–36.

Reflection: St. Luke's version above is, typically, the only one which explicitly mentions that Jesus "went up onto a mountain to pray and while he was praying. . . ." We say typically because St. Luke does frequently mention incidents during which Jesus is at prayer. Thus our Lord offers us here a study in and model of prayerfulness.

But the transfiguration account also points to Christ as a model for us in all our other activities. Listen to him, listen to my beloved Son, the biblical text reads.

Silent Period of Meditation
Prayer for Eucharistic Ministers

SET 4: FILLED WITH FAITH

FIRST DAY

Patron Saint: St. Thomas the apostle. Just as it can be encouraging to us that Jesus chose weak Peter as the rock foundation and leader of the Church, so the selection of Thomas, a skeptic, may be comforting for us. In the incident we will read below, this follower of Christ earned the title of a "doubting Thomas," and that expression has been handed down from then until now.

Earlier (John 11:16) Thomas had displayed a generosity and openness to the Lord's direction when, in the discussion with Jesus about Lazarus, he said to his fellow disciples, "Let us go along, to die with him."

However, during Easter week and the Sunday after our Lord's resurrection, Thomas doubted and had to see to believe, to touch in order to become convinced that Jesus had risen.

Grace Sought: To have deep faith in Jesus and the Eucharist.

Scripture Reading: John 11:1–16; 20:19–29.

131

Reflection: We do not glorify the weakness of Peter or the skepticism of Thomas, but take courage from the evidence in those cases of how God understands our humanness and with grace transforms us.

St. Thomas' act of faith, "My Lord and my God," has become one of the familiar expressions of belief in Christianity. For years, too, Catholics were popularly taught to whisper these words silently at the elevation of Mass.

Eucharistic ministers should find that phrase and the faith of Thomas helpful to them in deepening their belief in the risen Lord's presence under the sign of bread and wine.

Silent Period of Meditation
Prayer for Eucharistic Ministers

SECOND DAY

Patron Saint: St. Joseph. This good man was constantly asked by God to trust, to believe, to have faith, to follow a path that seemed strange and unclear.

He was engaged to Mary, but before they lived together as husband and wife she became pregnant, and the angel said: "Have no fear of taking Mary as your wife."

After the child had been born, an angel of the Lord again gave sudden directions, "Get up, take the child and his mother, and flee to Egypt."

Following Herod's death, the messenger returned with more orders, "Get up, take the child and his mother, and set out for the land of Israel."

The promptness of his response in all these cases reflects Joseph's deep faith and sure trust in God.

"When Jesus awoke he did as the angel of the Lord had directed him. . . ."

132

"Joseph got up and took the child and his mother and left that night for Egypt."

"He got up, took the child and his mother, and returned to the land of Israel."

No hesitation, no questioning. "That night" he got up and followed directions.

Grace Sought: To be prompt in following God's will and to die in the Lord's arms.

Scripture Reading: Matthew 1:18–2:23.

Reflection: Joseph held the Christ child in his arms, believed in the Lord's word, cared for son and mother, and probably died in their embrace.

He established a pattern we can try to imitate and experienced an end we hope to enjoy.

Silent Period of Meditation
Prayer for Eucharistic Ministers

THIRD DAY

Patron Saint: St. Clare. In the early part of the twelfth century, this teenage girl fell in love with two people: Christ and St. Francis. The latter led her to the former and inspired Clare to leave all things for the Lord.

That was a faith decision, one which caused her enormous pain, lifelong suffering and many tears. At the convent of San Damiano in Assisi she founded a cloistered community of nuns we call today the Poor Clares, a companion contemplative body to the group founded by her beloved Francis.

Clare's life was simple and austere, filled with prayer, but very much in tune with life on the outside. The joy and holiness of her sisters attracted those beyond the walls to come frequently for help and counsel, and even to be healed by her laying on of hands.

133

Her inner life centered on the Eucharist and there she found comfort in the midst of anguish over her wealthy father's lifelong refusal to forgive Clare for leaving home and following the Lord.

She believed that at least after death both would be reconciled and he would understand.

Grace Sought: To be detached.

Scripture Reading: Matthew 19:16–30; Mark 10:17–31; Luke 18:18–30.

Reflection: Clare's faith led her to renounce all possessions, live poorly, and serve Christ in others by that life. Most eucharistic ministers are lay persons, people who must live in the world. They, too, are called to follow Christ in faith with a spirit of simplicity and poverty. But the word for them is detachment, not renunciation.

In the words of one writer, this means to use creatures joyfully without guilt, but to be deprived of them without a sense of loss.

Religious who renounce all usually have more security than lay persons who retain things, but constantly risk losing all.

In either option, faith in the Lord and his call dictates the style of life we lead. That approach of renunciation or detachment will speak to others about our belief in Christ and make our ministry with the Eucharist more credible to those we serve.

Silent Period of Meditation
Prayer for Eucharistic Ministers

SET 5: REACHING OUT

FIRST DAY

Patron Saint: St. Lawrence. Like many of the early saints, we know very little about this man who was a deacon in the Church of Rome. However, his imitation of Christ during life and heroic example in death as a martyr led those first Christians quickly to judge Lawrence a saint. By the fourth century devotion to him had spread throughout the Church, and in the revised calendar his celebration as a feast ranks higher than those of ordinary martyrs. His position as a deacon, after the model described in the Acts of the Apostles and exemplified by Stephen, meant that St. Lawrence's efforts were directed primarily to the poor, the widows, and the orphaned. Placed in charge of the Church treasury, he was vulnerable to attacks by Roman officials who looked with covetous eyes to what they judged an immense prize.

Fearing such confiscation, Lawrence distributed all available assets, including chalices, to the poor. Later when asked to bring forth the Church's wealth, he assembled the poor, aged, sick and orphans and announced, "Here is the treasury of our Church."

Legend has it that the furious official then consigned him to a slow, cruel death through roasting on a gridiron. Tradition also mentions that after a period of burning, St. Lawrence lightheartedly remarked, "One side is well done now; why not turn me over?"

Grace Sought: To be cheerful givers and willing sharers of our resources with others.

Scripture Reading: 2 Corinthians 9:6–10; John 12:24–26.

Reflection: Contemporary heroes who inspire us with their unselfish service of others, like Mother Teresa of Calcutta, radiate a cheerfulness, a joy, a contentment with their lives.

These two biblical passages, used for the feast of St. Lawrence on August 10, mirror his life and these modern-day servants of charity as well.

135

Silent Period of Meditation
Prayer for Eucharistic Ministers

SECOND DAY

Patron Saint: Father Damien the leper. During the second half of the last century, this husky, athletic, enthusiastic missionary asked his superiors for permission to work with the isolated victims of leprosy on Molokai in the Hawaiian islands. The bishop granted this wish, and from 1873–1889 the Belgian priest labored on that small bit of land which juts out into the ocean.

The stories of his few years reveal a heroic man consumed with love for God, the Church and the hurting. He addressed his flock from the beginning with the words, "We lepers," even though Damien did not contract the dreaded disease until later; he built churches, constructed a water system, buried the dead, cared for the sick, taught the children, and served as policeman, judge and lawyer; eventually his body, too, wasted away and claimed the life of a man whose tombstone by the chapel he built reads: "A victim of charity."

There are only a few lepers left at Molokai, a dozen or so in the hospital and perhaps a few hundred on the settlement. The World War II sulfa drugs, it was found, could control the disease's hideous effects. But a visitor can still see some of its ravages—a man with two wooden legs and stumps for hands, an older blind woman with cramped fingers who prays the rosary with her mouth.

In Damien's day, the sights were horrendous, the odors nauseating, the prospects dismal and hopeless. Yet Father Damien rose above his natural revulsion and continued to serve them. He touched and embraced them, an essential sign to Hawaiians of one's sincere love, despite the understandable hesitation or reluctance. Damien saw Christ in them.

His cause for canonization is being pursued in Rome.

Grace Sought: To see Christ in our communicants, especially those who are ill or in any way offensive.

Scripture Reading: Matthew 25:31–46.

Reflection: Some Scripture scholars today question if this passage has as general a message as we traditionally give to it. They argue that the Lord speaks here specifically about those he is sending out to preach, the persons who are his followers or disciples. Brothers, in that context, refers to them. During the past decades, however, we have tended to quote this in support of our obligation to show love and concern for all hurting people.

Regardless of that discussion, the text presents an ideal or a model for eucharistic ministers. To see Jesus in those who come before us at the altar, to recognize the Lord in the sick persons at home or hospital who receive Communion from our hands—such an approach can help overcome the natural failings and lack of enthusiasm which result from routine.

Silent Period of Meditation
Prayer for Eucharistic Ministers

THIRD DAY

Patron Saint: St. Elizabeth Ann Seton. Born at the time of the American Revolution, our saint was reared a staunch Episcopalian, married at nineteen, bore five children and at thirty was widowed and penniless.

During a stay in Italy she became a Catholic and developed three inner traits: belief in the Real Presence, devotion to the Blessed Mother, and conviction that the Catholic Church led back to the apostles and to Christ.

She suffered great rejections, opened Catholic schools, founded a religious community and was proclaimed in September 1975 the first American-born citizen to be canonized a saint.[4]

Grace Sought: To have our love for the Blessed Sacrament flow over into our love for others.

Scripture Reading: Matthew 19:13–15; Mark 10:13–16; Luke 18:15–17.

Reflection: Priests, deacons and eucharistic ministers who bless infants and pre-First Communion children at the altar with a hand imposed and some kind of simple formula like "May the body of Christ soon come into your heart" may look to these Gospel excerpts for support of that practice.

Christ's words about becoming like children refer, in the opinion of some commentators, to their powerlessness and not their innocence. Young boys and girls may not always be innocent, but they are helpless and dependent. Our stance before God should be the same.

Mother Seton's great love for the Eucharist and her devotion in prayer to the Blessed Sacrament overflowed into service of others, especially children. She thus serves in that way as a model for all eucharistic ministers.

Silent Period of Meditation
Prayer for Eucharistic Ministers

Notes

INTRODUCTION

1. *Study Text I, Holy Communion.* Bishops' Committee on the Liturgy. Washington, D.C.: United States Catholic Conference, 1973, p. 37.

2. *Ibid.*, p. 3.

CHAPTER 1

1. Rev. Joseph A. Jungmann, S.J., *The Mass of the Roman Rite.* New York: Benziger Brothers, Inc., 1959, pp. 498–510.

2. *The Body of Christ.* Published by the Bishops' Committee on the Liturgy. Washington: U.S.C.C. Publications Office, 1977, pp. 11–15. This booklet with its compilation of official documents on the Eucharist issued in recent years includes an adaptation of an excellent historical overview of Communion in the hand by Archbishop Annibale Bugnini, then Secretary of the Congregation for Worship which originally appeared in *L'Osservatore Romano* (English translation: *Origins*, August 15, 1973).

139

CHAPTER 2

1. R. Kevin Seasoltz, *The New Liturgy: A Documentation 1903 to 1965.* New York: Herder and Herder, 1966. This Benedictine scholar in his lengthy introduction presents a brief, but thorough and interesting historical overview of the contemporary liturgical movement. The text itself contains the salient official documents on the liturgy which have appeared during this period. My quotations from such decrees are generally excerpted from his volume.

2. *Ibid.*, pp. xxvi–xxvii.

3. *Ibid.*, p. 86.

4. *Ibid.*, p. 91.

5. *Ibid.*

6. *Ibid.*, p. 131.

7. *Ibid.*, p. 478.

8. *Ibid.*, p. 481.

9. *Ibid.*

10. *Study Text I, Holy Communion.* Bishop's Committee on the Liturgy. Washington, D.C., United States Catholic Conference, 1979, pp. 3–10.

11. *Ibid.*, p. 12.

12. This section of the Roman Ritual entitled *Holy Communion and Worship of the Eucharist Outside of Mass* has been divided into three distinct booklets published by the United States Catholic Conference, 1312 Massachusetts Avenue, N.W., Washington, D.C. 20005: *Holy Communion Outside of Mass, Administration of Communion and Viaticum to the Sick by an Extraordinary Minister,* and *Forms of Worship of the Eucharist: Exposition, Benediction, Processions, Congresses.*.

13. Study *Text I, op. cit.*, p. 3.

CHAPTER 3

1. Matthew 9:35–38. New American Bible translation.

2. Matthew 10:1–5.

3. Luke 6:12–13.

4. Mark 3:13–15.
5. Acts 1:15–26.
6. Acts 6:1–6.
7. Exodus 18:13–25; Deuteronomy 1:9–18.
8. *Holy Communion Outside of Mass, op. cit.,* p. 7, article 14. See reference ch. 2, footnote 12.
9. *Study Text I, op. cit.,* p. 5.
10. *Ibid.,* p. 5.
11. *Rite of Commissioning Special Ministers of Holy Communion, ICEL,* 1978, pp. 9–13.

CHAPTER 4

1. *The Order of Mass.*

CHAPTER 5

1. *The Documents of Vatican II,* Walter M. Abbott, S.J., General Editor. New York: The America Press, 1966. "Decree on the Ministry and Life of Priests," article 12.
2. Matthew 26:40.
3. Matthew 26:41.
4. 2 Corinthians 12:7–10.
5. *Holy Communion Outside of Mass, op. cit.,* p. 4, article 6.
6. *Ibid.,* p. 3, article 1.
7. *Ibid.,* p. 3, article 2.
8. Luke 10:42.
9. *Music in Catholic Worship,* Bishops' Committee on the Liturgy. Washington, D.C.: United States Catholic Conference, 1972, p. 1, article 1.
10. *Ibid.,* p. 1, article 4.
11. *Ibid.,* p. 1, article 6.
12. *Ibid.,* p. 4, article 21.
13. Exodus 3:1–6.
14. *Holy Communion Outside of Mass, op. cit.,* p. 3, article 3.

15. *Forms of Worship of the Eucharist: Exposition, Benediction, Processions, Congresses, op. cit.,* p. 7, articles 80–81.

16. *Holy Communion Outside of Mass, op. cit.,* p. 10, article 25.

17. *Ibid.,* p. 10, article 25.

18. *Selected Documentation from the Sacramentary.* Washington, D.C.: USCC Publications Office, 1974, p. 42, article 60.

19. Luke 2:10.

20. Luke 24:40–41.

21. Acts 2:46–47.

22. Galatians 5:22.

23. 1 Thessalonians 5:16.

24. *Music in Catholic Worship, op. cit.,* p. 1, article 5.

25. *Holy Communion Outside of Mass, op. cit.,* pp. 9–10, article 23.

26. *Ibid.,* p. 10, article 24.

27. *Study Text I, op. cit.,* p. 15.

28. *Selected Documentation from the Sacramentary, op. cit.,* pp. 28–29, Chapter I.

29. *Ibid.,* pp. 40–41, articles 56, 56i.

CHAPTER 7

1. *Study Text I, op. cit.,* p. 16.

2. *Ibid.,* p. 5.

3. *Rite of Commissioning Special Ministers of Holy Communion, op. cit.*

4. *Study Text I, op. cit.,* p. 15.

5. *Ibid.*

6. *Ibid.,* p. 40.

7. *Holy Communion Outside of Mass, op. cit.,* p. 21, article 36.

8. *Study Text I, op. cit.,* p. 45.

9. *Administration of Communion and Viaticum to the Sick by an Extraordinary Minister, op. cit.,* p. 13, article 62.

10. *Study Text I, op. cit.,* p. 40.

11. *Ibid.*, p. 15.

12. *Ibid.*, p. 13.

13. *Rite of Commissioning Special Ministers of Holy Communion, op. cit.*, pp. 13–15.

CHAPTER 8

1. Matthew 26:26–29; Mark 14:22–25; Luke 22:14–20; 1 Corinthians 11:23 ff.

2. *The Body of Christ, op. cit.*, pp. 26–29. My above historical treatment of Communion from the cup has been taken almost verbatim, with minor editing, from that text published by the Bishops' Committee on the Liturgy. The original booklet includes a half-dozen footnotes referring to official documents from which statements have been made or adapted.

3. *Ibid.*, p. 28. Here, too, we have excerpted a section verbatim with only minor editing.

4. Mark 10:35–38.

5. Matthew 26:36–46; Mark 14:32–42.

6. 1 Corinthians 10:21.

7. Eucharistic Prayer III.

8. Eucharistic Prayer IV.

9. Theodore of Mopsuestia, *Catechetical Homilies*, quoted in *Newsletter* from the Bishops' Committee on the Liturgy, Volume XIV, October 1978, pp. 135–136.

10. *Selected Documentation from the Sacramentary, op. cit.*, p. 77, articles 290–291; p. 96, article 288.

11. *Environment and Art in Catholic Worship*, Bishops' Committee on the Liturgy. Washington, D.C.: USCC Publications Office, 1978, pp. 14–15, article 20.

12. *Ibid.*, p. 47, article 96.

CHAPTER 9

1. *Holy Communion Outside of Mass, op. cit.*, p. 7, article 14.

2. *Ibid.*
3. *Administration of Communion and Viaticum to the Sick by an Extraordinary Minister, op. cit.*
4. *Holy Communion Outside of Mass, op. cit.*, p. 7, article 14.
5. *Administration of Communion and Viaticum to the Sick by an Extraordinary Minister, op. cit.*, pp. 7–16.
6. *Ibid.*, pp. 17–21.
7. *Ibid.*, pp. 22–29.
8. Joseph M. Champlin, *Together by Your Side.* Notre Dame, Indiana: Ave Maria Press, 1979.

CHAPTER 10

1. *Study Text I, op. cit.*, p. 4.
2. *General Instruction, Liturgy of the Hours*, Section VII, articles 93–99.
3. *Holy Communion Outside of Mass, op. cit.*, pp. 13–26.

CHAPTER 11

1. *Selected Documentation from the Sacramentary, op. cit.*, p. 42, article 60.
2. We wish to credit with thanks this prayer to: Mr. and Mrs. John Fusco, 102 Trinity Place, Hillsdale, New Jersey 07642.
3. Acts 6:5.
4. *Saint of the Day*, edited by Leonard Foley, O.F.M. Cincinnati: St. Anthony Messenger Press, 1974, Volume I, pp. 5–7. This two-volume paperback series would be a helpful companion for the eucharistic minister who participates frequently in daily Mass.